voices from ROBBEN ISLAND

Compiled and
Photographed by
JÜRGEN SCHADEBERG

Published by Ravan Press (Pty) Ltd
P O Box 145 Randburg 2125
South Africa

First published 1994.

ISBN 0 86975 454 8 softback
ISBN 0 86975 455 6 hardback

Cover design: Ingrid Obery, Ravan Press and Centre Court Studio
Design: Jürgen Schadeberg
DTP: Centre Court Studio
Editor: Ingrid Obery, Ravan Press
Research: Claudia Schadeberg

Acknowledgements:

Material for the history of Robben Island is largely drawn from work done for the Mayibuye Centre and the South African Museum's 'Esiqithini: The Robben Island Exhibition' by Patricia Davidson, André Odendaal, Harriet Deacon, Nigel Penn, Melissa Stander and Gerald Klinghardt.

Robben Island, by Mary Benson:

Dennis Brutus gave permission for quotations from his poems.
Indris Naidoo gave permission for the adaptation of extracts from his book *Island in Chains,* Benjamin Pogrund gave permission for the use of material from his book *Sobukwe,* R. Vigne gave permission for the use of text from *Robben Island* by D M Swelenke. Historical information was drawn from the following texts:
R Raven-Hart, *Before Van Riebeeck: Caller at SA 1488-1652,* Struik 1967
R B Thorn, *Journal of Van Riebeeck,* Balkema, 1952-8
S de Villiers, *Robben Island,* Struik, 1971
H E Hockley, *The Story of the British Settlers of 1820 in SA,* Juta 1948

Printed by Penrose Printers

CONTENTS

Island of the Damned

Deep into the icy waters of the Atlantic
Somewhere around the Cape of Storms
encaged by rocky beaches all round
assaulted by piercing winds from the Benguelo
like an abandoned ship... lies the Island of the damned.

There it was where colonial vehicles crashed
on their infamous voyage of theft and plunder,
to rob the priceless treasures of Monomotapa
leaving a bloody trail to mark their mission—
Thaba Bosiu, Isandlwana, Bambatha.

The house of Ndlambe was razed
the babes of Shaka were routed
the tears of Sekhukhune filled valleys
the blood of Moshoeshoe cried murder!
as Makana lay chained on the Island of the damned.

The 1912 overture sounded near and far
summoning marshalls and generals to one table
joining the children of Africa under one flag
there to plan one strategy — one command
for the alignment of all fighting forces.

Umkhonto we Sizwe today is the battle cry
rallying all to answer the clarion call
vakani izwe lifile it says to all
as the gallant fighters to arms take
fingers are crossed on the Island of the damned.

All victims of the leper are locked there
the germ-carrier roams freely outside
seeking new innocents to suck new blood
yet soon the monster will be crushed
and life never will the same be again
even on the Island and of the damned!

Tokyo M. G. Sexwale.
Robben Island 1979.

Robben Island, meaning Island of Seals, was given its name by Dutch navigators in the sixteenth century. At that time the mainland was populated by the Khoikhoi, whom the Dutch thought were cannibals. Robben Island on the other hand was seen as a safe refreshment stop for sailors, where they could dine indefinitely on seal steaks, penguin meat and penguin eggs.

On a clear day Robben Island is visible from Cape Town's shore. The swimming pool at Seapoint on a hot summer's day. Now swimmers and sun-worshippers of all races run, jump, scream and laugh, oblivious of the narrow piece of land just eight miles out to sea where hundreds of political prisoners spent decades fighting for this new-found freedom.

Introduction

The history of Robben Island is largely unknown to the majority of South Africans. The name conjures up pictures of a dark, sinister, desolate place which was isolated from normal life. Those incarcerated there were meant to be silenced for ever and forgotten.

For the last 400 years, Robben Island has been used as a dumping ground for those deemed to be a social or political threat to society. Like the notorious American prison Alcatraz, Robben Island was reputed to be a high security prison from which there was no escape.

Ever since the arrival of the first white settlers at the Cape in the fifteenth century, people were banished to the Island: Khoikhoi accused of petty theft, Xhosa chiefs who opposed British imperialism, British convicts, the mentally ill who were described as lunatics, and those suffering from leprosy.

In 1960 the Afrikaner Nationalist Government made Robben Island a high security prison. They used the prison to isolate black, coloured and Indian political prisoners who opposed the Apartheid regime.

In 1964, the Rivonia trialists were sent to Robben Island. These leaders were kept in single cells in a section isolated from the hundreds of other men who, in one way or another, opposed the system — MK soldiers, youth leaders, ANC or PAC members, and those who had been caught with anti-Apartheid pamphlets or documents.

This concentration of political activists from a variety of political affiliations had the effect over the years and decades of creating a powerful, disciplined and united political force both inside and outside the prison. This force impacted on the national and international scene and could not be repressed by the regime.

Under the leadership of Nelson Mandela and Walter Sisulu, the prison on Robben Island became a symbol, not only for the worldwide struggle against Apartheid, but also a centre of learning. Hundreds of political prisoners studied a variety of subjects, often to degree stage, gaining their BAs and MAs from universities such as UNISA. This disciplined and dynamic nucleus of people eventually became central in determining South Africa's smooth transition to a new political era.

The many stories of human suffering, hardship, courage and defiance, of perseverance and patience on the Island are still to be told. These stories must not be lost, and should be documented for future generations so that they can learn from the unyielding determination of the prisoners of Robben Island.

This book would not have been possible without the help of a number of people. Claudia Schadeberg, my wife and partner, this year produced a 90 minute documentary film about the history of Robben Island. This co-production with the BBC was entitled *Voices from Robben Island,* and much of the material for this book was taken from our film. My appreciation to Claudia for her tenacity, persistence and determination to make our Robben Island project a reality.

Our director, Adam Low, conducted the interviews for the film, and extracts from these interviews are used in the book. Elinor Sisulu accompanied the film crew on our visit to Robben Island with Albertina and Walter Sisulu and June and Andrew Mlangeni, and wrote about her impressions of that memorable return visit to the Island. Enoch Sithole and I went to Robben Island on 11th February 1994 when Nelson Mandela revisited the prison with six other Rivonia trialists. Charlene Smith from Radio 702 contributed the piece on escapes from Robben Island. I would like to thank Mary Benson for allowing us to publish her radio play about Robben Island.

Many thanks and appreciation to Ingrid Obery from Ravan Press for her professional advice and encouragement. I would also like to thank Dr Ivan May of Nedbank for his invaluable support and for recognising the historical importance of documenting *Voices From Robben Island.* And of course our thanks to all the Islanders who generously shared with us their often painful stories of their years on Robben Island.

Jürgen Schadeberg
June 1994

Robben Island
A Brief History

Walk down the street, a dusty pot-holed tar road, and a gust of wind blows sand in your face. A sinister looking church, its windows boarded up, is flanked by two ancient cannon. A small flag flutters from the church tower, which resembles a castle turret. It cracks and snaps in the wind. The pavement is made up of seashells and pebbles which crunch under your feet. Rows of tin-roofed houses are surrounded by short stone walls.

Crossing Barrack Road you see an abandoned car — a 20-year-old Peugeot, its bonnet eaten away by rust, with the driver's door missing. It has lost its number plate and its former red colour is now a dull, pale brown.

Except for the occasional burst of howling and whining wind along the main road there is total silence. The Island seems deserted, the only activity the swaying of an occasional fir tree and the thin clouds scudding across the misty pale blue sky.

A figure appears from one of the larger buildings, the general store, which bears a sign high above the windows: 'Enjoy Coke — Robben Eiland Ledewinkel'. The man walks briskly towards the car wreck. He is dressed in a khaki uniform and a ribbed jersey with epaulettes, his trousers tucked into his parabat boots. He wears a small-brimmed soft hat. The figure climbs into the wreck and with a tremendous banging, coughing and spluttering, the car speeds down the main street.

Now there are sounds of children laughing and shouting, then silence again. Forty-two white children in their blue school uniforms stand to attention in front of a nineteenth century Victorian building. They raise the old South African flag and sing the national anthem, *Die Stem*. Slowly the flag rises to the top of the flagpole.

Passing the club house, an impressive mock Tudor building flanked by two large anchors, you can see the mountains of Cape Town with the top of Table Mountain covered in clouds. Walking down a sandy path in the direction of Cape Town, clumps of tall straw-coloured grass and the occasional green bush bend and dance in the driving wind. At the shore, beds of rocks are pounded by the sea. Robben Island is separated from the mainland by eight miles of rough, cold Atlantic Ocean.

Robben Island was not always an island, geologists claim. Rising and falling sea-levels changed its face, and in the past 700 000 years alone there were 12 periods

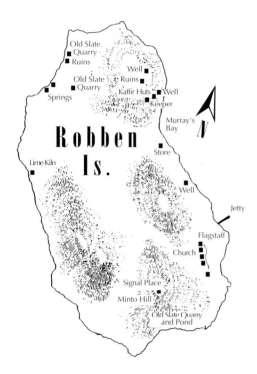

of lower sea levels during which times the Island would have been linked to the mainland. Archeological evidence shows that early tool makers lived in the Western Cape hundreds of thousands of years ago, and although no direct evidence of early human use of the Island has yet been found, it would no doubt have been familiar territory to these ancient peoples. After the Ice Age, about 12 000 years ago, rising sea levels again cut the Island off from the mainland. Since that time, apart from a further rise in the sea level, it has remained largely unchanged.

Robben Island is two kilometres wide, three-and-a-half kilometres long and is comprised largely of rock and sand. This 'Isle of Purgatory at the foot of Paradise' is separated from the mainland by icy, stormy waters. The top of Table Mountain was named Paradise by European writers in the mid-sixteenth century, after Portuguese explorers returned to Europe with news of the Cape of Good Hope.

From 1488, when Bartolemeu Dias anchored in Table Bay, there are records of several Portuguese ships visiting the Cape, and the Island. There were no humans on Robben Island, but there were tens of thousands of seals and penguins, which provided an unlimited supply of food to mariners for the next two centuries.

In 1503 Antonio de Saldanha and his men 'killed many birds (penguins) and sea-wolves (seals) and tortoises, of which there was great abundance' on the Island. This slaughter was to accelerate throughout the sixteenth and into the seventeenth century as more and more ships made the long return voyage from the East and came to rely on this half-way point to replenish their supplies. Throughout this time it became a practice to leave sheep on the Island in the hope that they would multiply and provide food for future trips.

Robben Island was also believed to be safer and more reliable for stocking up on fresh food supplies. The Island was devoid of humans, unlike the mainland where the Khoikhoi lived. In 1510 Francisco d'Almeida and 50 of his men were killed after trying to steal Khoikhoi cattle and kidnap Khoikhoi children. Indeed, the Khoikhoi were not always keen to barter their precious cattle and goats in exchange for European glass jewels, mirrors and iron trinkets.

In 1608 some English sailors found 'penguins to be so simple-minded that you may drive them as you would a flock of sheep'. They laid boards from the beach to their boat and herded the 'feathered fish' into it. No wonder the English called it Penguin Island. The Dutch however called it Seal Island or Sea-Dog Island from

the Dutch word for seal — *robbe*. The seals were as numerous as the penguins. In 1608 Dutch Admiral Cornelius Matelief described these 'sea-dogs' as having 'lovely pelts'. For their amusement, his men clubbed 'fully 100 to death'.

The first record of the Island being used as a place of banishment is 1525, when a Portuguese ship is said to have left some convicts there. It is not known what became of them. The next group of convicts arrived on Robben Island in 1615. The English East India Company attempted to establish a settlement of convicts in the Cape. Ten arrived, under the leadership of John Cross, a convicted highway robber who had been sentenced to hang. Just days after the convicts landed they were attacked by Khoikhoi, who seriously wounded four of the group. Fortunately the English ship *Hope* was in Table Bay, and Cross begged its skipper, Edward Dodsworth, to provide them with guns and a longboat so that they could withdraw to the safety of Robben Island.

The first 'official' on Robben Island was Harry, or Autshumao, a Khoikhoi who worked for the East India Company. Autshumao was originally the leader of a group of cattleless Khoikhoi known as *Strandlopers*. In 1631 he was taken on a voyage to the East Indies where he learnt to speak English. A year later he was posted to Robben Island with 20 of his followers and took up the position of agent and postmaster for the East India Company. He stayed there until 1640 monitoring all the ships that entered the bay and lighting signal fires. He lived a secure life away from the often hostile Khoikhoi on the mainland. In 1634 a traveller to Robben Island, Peter Mundy, described Autshumao as 'Chief of all that dwell there and Governor of the Island'.

In 1652 Jan van Riebeeck arrived and set about establishing a permanent settlement at the Cape. Autshumao played the vital role of middle man and translator between the Khoikhoi and the Dutch. However in 1658 Van Riebeeck grew suspicious of Autshumao and banished him and two Khoikhoi companions Jan Coo and Boubo, to Robben Island. They were, in effect, the Island's first 'political prisoners'. In 1659 Autshumao escaped from the Island by boat and by 1660 was back on the mainland working for the Dutch.

Autshumao and his men were not the first to be banished to Robben Island by the colonial authorities. In May 1657 a decision was made to send slaves and exiles there to work in the lime quarry to cut and prepare this soft white stone. Under the command of the Postholder, Jan Wouterssen, those sent there included Thomas Mulder, a company servant, Jasper Duijff, a banished soldier, Lourens

Lijst der gecondemneerde Europianen op 't Robben EyLandt — handwritten list of names with places, dates, and durations.

Alberts, an exile, Espagniola, a slave, and Eva, a slave from Madagascar. This whole exercise proved to be a total failure as the Postholder documented on 19th July 1657: 'The stone was too crumbly and many of the men became ill — Lourens Alberts contracted beri-beri, Jasper Duijff had Ceylon disease — while Eva did nothing but run around the Island chasing sheep'.

A steady trickle of convicts, sentenced to hard labour, came to the Island. Apart from working in the lime quarry they had the added task of digging for blue stone. In 1677 the then Commander of Robben Island, Wagenaar, wrote, '... for the Island makes a very good penitentiary where a rogue, after one of two years work in carrying shells, begins to sing very small'. The need for lime and slate had grown and increasing numbers of convicts were banished to the Island.

During the eighteenth century the Island was used as a dumping ground for political dissidents resistant to the East India company: high-ranking exiles from the East, Muslim priests, Chinese, Madagascans, Indian slaves, Khoikhoi, pirates and robbers. The Dutch called black prisoners 'Indiaanen bandieten'.

In 1744 two Muslim holy men — Said Akloeurie and Hadje Mattarm — were banished to the Island, and since that time Robben Island has been regarded as one of the crucibles for the consolidation of Islam in Southern Africa.

In 1749 Daing Mangenam, Prince of Macasser, was exiled to the Island. He was allowed to receive ten rixdollars a month to help pay for his keep. Less fortunate convicts were subject to harsh beatings and other brutal forms of punishment.

A group of 'Indiaanen bandieten' mutinied in 1751. They conspired to kill all the Europeans and capture the provisions boat so that they could sail to the East Indies. But Sergeant Frederick Hofman caught one of the conspirators, September van Ternaten, stealing some money and, after a severe beating, September confessed everything. Many of the conspirators tried to implicate Prince Daing Mangenam but he denied involvement, saying that he had no reason

Xhosa Chief Siyola, son of Mdushane, was sent to Robben Island in May 1855. He was released in 1869.

Photograph: Gustav Fritsch

to be party to such a plot since the Company gave him everything he needed. Sergeant Hofman supported the Prince. Six of the conspirators ended up with broken bodies tied to crude crosses while a further three were hanged.

The 'Bandieten Rollen', a list of all the prisoners, was discontinued in 1806 and all convicts were removed to the Amsterdam Battery on the mainland. The following year the British returned prisoners to Robben Island, including military convicts, who continued to work in the slate quarries.

In 1819 the Xhosa prophet Makana, who was also known as Nxele or Makhanda, was banished to the Island. Makana had rallied forces against the British who had begun a campaign to destroy the Ngqikas. In 1819 the Gcaleka and Ndlambe combined to attack the British at Grahamstown. This provoked the colonists to drive the Xhosa across the Fish River, which they had been trying to do for some time. Makhanda surrendered in an attempt to make peace — his people were starving, their crops burnt and their stock dying. In 1820 Makana and 300 others escaped from the Island in three boats. Only four survived the high seas off Bloubergstrand.

The Colonial Medical Committee reported in 1842 that Robben Island would be an ideal location for the reception, seclusion and proper treatment of persons afflicted with leprosy. In 1846 Dr John Birtwhistle came from England to be the Resident Surgeon on Robben Island, and the existing prison buildings were turned into hospital wards. By 1847, 194 lepers, lunatics and the chronic sick had arrived on the Island. Women and men were kept apart but there was no racial segregation, nor any seperation of the lepers from the other patients.

In 1852 a Government Commission of Enquiry began to investigate allegations of mismanagement and the ill-treatment of patients on Robben Island. Dr Birtwhistle's method of forcible restraint by chaining and beating patients was considered outdated. Three years later Birtwhistle was dismissed for malpractice and embezzling funds.

Dilima ama Ndhlambe, son of Chief Phato of the Khoi-Xhosa clan, sent to Robben Island in 1858.

Photograph: Gustav Fritsch

There was a court case in Cape Town in 1858 which focused attention on the continuing cruel treatment of mental patients on the Island, which led to the increase in public criticism. At this time there were 396 patients on the Island and 19 staff members. In 1862 a Dr William Edmunds became surgeon-superintendent and implemented more enlightened policies.

During the mid-nineteenth century the grip of colonialism tightened over the Xhosa, and many tribal leaders ended up on the Island. Xhosa Chief Siyolo was sent to Robben Island in May 1855 after the 'War of Mlangene' against the British in protest against the loss of independence. Siyolo was accompanied by his wife and they were imprisoned in a house in the village, which was a separate section of the female leper asylum. Siyolo was released in 1869. He joine d forces with the Ngqika people in the last Frontier War and was shot dead by the British.

Several other Xhosa chiefs were imprisoned on Robben Island after another Xhosa offensive against the British — Maqoma, one of Chief Ngqika's sons, Maqoma's brother Xhoxho, and Chief Mhala and his son Dilima.

Maqoma and Xhoxho were also released in 1869 and returned home. Maqoma, however, tried to reoccupy his land near Fort Beaufort in the Ciskei which had been taken by the British while he was on the Island, and he was returned to Robben Island in 1871. He died on Robben Island in September 1873, a weak and lonely old man whose home was the stark pauper ward.

In 1874 the Hlubi Chief Langalibalele arrived on Robben Island. The Hlubi had been relocated by Sir Theophilus Shepstone to the upper stretches of the Bushman's River near the Drakensberg to form a buffer between the San in the Drakensberg Range and the colonists. Langalibalele's influence as a visionary grew and his following increased. He became a threat to the colonists and Shepstone's 'Bantu Policy', and troops were sent in to capture him. He managed to escape to Lesotho where he was arrested by the British and put on trial. Langalibalele's lawyer withdrew from the trial in protest as he was given no assurance that British law would prevail. Langalibalele was convicted of treason, murder and rebellion, although there was little evidence to support these charges.

In 1866 a branch station of the Breakwater convict station on Cape Town's waterfront was established on Robben Island. Long-term convicts from the Island were sent there to do hard labour in the docks. This practice continued until the 1920s.

Somi Amaponda, First Council of Sandhilli. Robben Island 1863-66

Photograph: Gustav Fritsch

*Group of nine chiefs on Robben Island
Maqoma seated on right, 1863.
Photograph: A Green*

*Chiefs Maqoma, Seyalo and Xhoxho after their
release from Robben Island, from a carte-de-
visite by William Moore, 1869.*

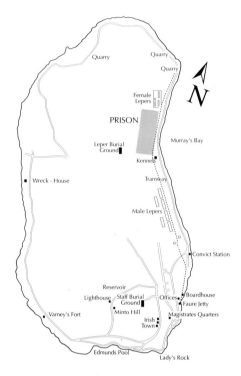

Robben Island c. 1898. This map shows where the prison is now situated.

Leper Patient.
Photograph: SA Library

The so-called lunatics on Robben Island often arrived via the courts and their families. Some were declared insane after being accused of a crime, others were picked off the streets as prostitutes, vagrants, drunks or suspected criminals. Some families requested that their relatives be sent to the Robben Island asylum if they were too violent, too expensive or too embarrassing.

One story tells of a Mrs Brown and her daughter who volunteered to go to Robben Island — the daughter had epilepsy and her mother suffered from a physical complaint. When they arrived they were bitterly disappointed because they were put in a large ward. They had no privacy and were constantly pestered by male lunatics. The food was poor and they had to wash their own clothes.

The chronic sick consisted mainly of destitute government employees, soldiers and sailors, many of whom were too old to work, ex-slaves who had been released from bondage in 1838 and could not support themselves, prostitutes and those with venereal diseases. The chronic sick were expected to look after each other. Then, with the increase in the numbers of lunatics, the sick were put to work and the threat of discharge loomed over their heads. Some became wardsmen and were paid a small fee.

In 1871, the female lepers were sent to the Old Somerset Hospital in Cape Town. They were returned to the Island in 1886 because fears arose that they were 'prostituting themselves' and therefore spreading the disease round Cape Town.

Fears increased in the Colony about the spread of leprosy, and Parliament passed the Leprosy Repression Act providing for the enforced segregation of all lepers within institutions. In 1887 lepers were prevented from visiting the mainland. Their protests to the Colonial Secretary were not heeded as leprosy was mistakenly believed to be highly contagious. In 1892 patients were admitted to a newly-built compound some distance from Robben Island village. Rigorous separation of lepers on the basis of race and sex was now enforced.

In her book *The Harp* published in the 1920s, Ethelreda Lewis wrote about Robben Island of the nineteenth century:

'In the leper compound sleep those whose minds are clear and bright, yet cloaked in flesh fatal and decayed. Simple minded gentle souls, only the brave and the pitying ever look them in the eyes with sweet, sustaining glance. But for these

General view of male leper settlement on Robben Island.
Photograph: Cape Archives

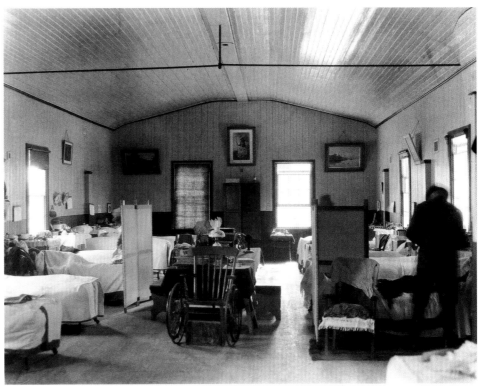

Interior of leper ward on Robben Island late nineteenth century.
Photograph: Cape Archives

A group of leper children with attendants.
Photograph: SA Library

blessed ones the lepers would often hunger and thirst for the bread and wine of human understanding. Then there is the asylum. There, in the wards and cells, lie beings of, it may be, fair and wholesome bodies whose minds yet wander in dread and darkness or in the fierce gleam of inner fires.

'There are other prisoners on the Island, in the convict station, where, too, are men who watch for light in the dark, brooding hours. For there is no prison safer than the Island. And all, all are caged that live there. All see the broad heavens striped with bars. All are held in unseen chains to the body, the mind, the soul. Even the captives on parole who walk at will in the lily-fields, who lie in the wattle-scented sunshine, or freely roam the jagged beach, even these fortunates are barred by rock and breaker and treacherous wind.'

In 1892 the lepers rebelled against the tight regime. The rebellion was led by a coloured leper named Franz Jacobs and under his leadership the lepers threatened to combine forces with the convicts. Jacobs wrote a petition to Queen Victoria complaining that they were treated like convicts. The lepers set fire to one of the wards and some attempted to escape. Extra men were brought onto the Island and employed as leper police and Jacobs was isolated from the Island community.

Nursing staff from the Women's Mental Asylum on Robben Island 1907.

Photograph: Cape Archives

The chronic sick left the Island in 1891, followed by the lunatics in 1921. In 1931 the lepers left the Island, and were sent to Westfort in Pretoria and Emjanyana in the Transkei. All buildings used by the lepers were burnt to the ground and the convict station was demolished. The population of the Island was reduced from two thousand to a handful of lighthouse keepers and labourers.

In 1936 Robben Island was declared a military reserve by the Minister of Defence, and in 1939 a fortification was constructed in preparation for war.

In 1960 Robben Island was taken over from the Department of Defence by the South African Prison Service and was once again opened as a jail for political prisoners. Members of Poqo, the ANC and SACP and other opposition groups were imprisoned on the Island from the early 1960s. PAC President Robert Sobukwe was held on the Island even after his sentence had expired. The General Law Amendment Act gave power to the prison authorities to prolong indefinitely the detention of any prisoner.

In 1964 Nelson Mandela and seven other leaders of the ANC and Umkhonto we Sizwe were sentenced to life imprisonment and sent to Robben Island. Conditions on Robben Island at this time were appalling — poor food, inadequate clothing,

severe punishments for minor transgressions and hard labour in the lime quarry. All the warders were white and all the prisoners were black. Something of their story is told in the pages that follow.

Over 30 years later, the prison and its immediate surroundings still appear ominous and threatening. A gateway into the prison area bears a large notice reading 'Welcome — Robbeneiland — Welkom — We serve with Pride — Ons dien met Trots'. One hundred metres up the road stands a large four wheeled cannon from the Second World War surrounded by neatly placed white bricks. A further 200 metres up the road is the prison, surrounded by rows of barbed wire, flanked by tall towers. The walls and the towers are covered with slate. Some way down the road, past low bushes surrounded by fencing, is an open piece of ground, 30 x 80 metres — the cemetery for lepers and other former inhabitants of the Island. Rows of unattended gravestones, some with elaborate designs, are broken and covered by drifting sand.

A few of the names and dates are still distinguishable. 'Paul Rossouw, born 8th February 1867, died 27th March 1911'. On another stone the only words remaining are 'Died 7th May 1890, aged 21 years'.

Voices
from the Island

Robben Island has become a symbol for the triumph of freedom over repression, a testament to the triumph of justice over injustice.

But it became so only through the suffering and hardship of those incarcerated behind its slate grey walls.

The following interviews with former Robben Island prisoners, their wives and warders, were conducted during November 1993 when we made a film about the history of the Island.

We selected extracts from the interviews which provided an overall picture, not only of the individual inverviewees and their different backgrounds, but also of prison conditions, reflecting all aspects of life on the Island. To some extent our choice was also guided by the availability of our interviewees, and we are very aware that time and space considerations meant that we were unable to include many other of the significant 'Voices from Robben Island'.

For most of the three decades of the recent political life of the prison, ANC prisoners made up 80% of the total number of prisoners. For some years in the early 1960s the number of political prisoners from other political groups such as the PAC rose. We have tried to reflect this proportion in our choice of interviews.

Ironically, and happily, most of the former inmates we interviewed are now either Members of Parliament or Provincial Government, Premiers of Regions, Senators or professionals. All have risen above, and built upon, their experiences on Robben Island.

The book is meant as a tribute to the courage and strength of all political prisoners who spent time on Robben Island, and who survived despite severe hardships. We also remember those prisoners who died on Robben Island, sacrificing their lives in the struggle for freedom.

Claudia Schadeberg

PRISONER 466/64
Nelson Mandela

PRISONER 466/64

What was important to us was the fact that the ideas for which we were sent to Robben Island would never die. It was a source of real encouragement to see that such ideas were winning new supporters and that the spirit of solidarity with our cause was visible... and growing.

This fed the hope that one day we would return. It enabled us to endure some of the harshest experiences a human being can have behind bars. On Robben Island the warders were drawn from a community which has always treated blacks like pieces of rags, and all the prisoners were black. Everything which enhanced your worth as a human being was suppressed... brutally suppressed. But we fought back and we won that battle.

Morale would ebb at times, especially when we were faced by the tactics of the regime, such as statements by heads of government that a life sentence meant life... that we would die in prison. Although we tried to keep our morale high there were moments of doubt... would our expectations be fulfilled so that one day we would return? It is only natural that there should have been moments of doubt.

In fact, despite divisions, all the different organisations gained tremendously from being together. The ANC was the largest, most experienced, group and we were therefore able to make a tremendous impact on the prison population, even on members of rival organisations.

And this vibrancy and difference was further enriched by the calibre of the men who were on the Island. It was fantastic, men with whom you could sit down and talk, and at the end of a conversation feel that you had been enriched, your horizons widened and your roots in your own country deepened. We realised that culture was a very important aspect to building a nation.

And sport was always important... it brings people of diverse views and talents together... it is one of the best ways of relaxing, of forgetting all the hard knocks of life... good exercise enables you to overcome any ailments you have. Big friendships were formed in the course of games. It is the desire of everybody in a team to win and there must be close co-operation. You must recognise the ability of the other sportsmen, as a striker, as a left-winger, as a fullback, as a goalie... and that cultivates a mutual respect and acceptance of the particular gifts of the individual. I played tennis and volleyball... and of course we had indoor games as well — chess, draughts, dominoes, scrabble... and monopoly was very popular.

We soon became aware that in terms of our daily lives a warder in our section, an ordinary warder, not a sergeant, could be more important to us than the Commissioner of Prisons or even the Minister of Justice. If you went to the Commissioner of Prisons or the Minister and said, 'Sir, it's very cold, I want four blankets', he would look at the regulations and say, 'You can only have three blankets... more would be a violation of the regulations, and if I give you four

Nelson Mandela was born on 18th July 1918. In 1964 he was charged with sabotage and conspiracy to overthrow the government by revolution. He was also charged with assisting an armed invasion of South Africa by foreign troops. Nelson Mandela was sentenced to life imprisonment on Robben Island on 13th June 1964. Eighteen years later, in April 1982, he was transferred to Pollsmoor Prison, in December 1988 to Victor Verster Prison, and he was released on 11th February 1990. Altogether he spent 27 years in prison. After the April 1994 elections, Mandela became President of South Africa.

'You are old or young depending on how you feel in your spirit ... you can put a lot of verve in you by the ideas you hold.'

blankets I'll have to give others four blankets'. If you went to a warder in your section and said, 'Look, I want an extra blanket', and if you treated him with respect, he'd just go to the storeroom, give you an extra blanket, and that's the end of it. If you said, 'Can I have some gravy today from the kitchen?'... he just went to the kitchen and got you gravy.

There were always warders who were exceptional and who treated us as human beings. We became aware that right from the beginning there was a raging debate, with some saying, 'Let's treat these people as human beings... we don't know what will happen in the future. It has happened on other occasions that people who have been prisoners are released and become heads of governments. Let us prepare for that day and let us give them newspapers, let us allow them radios'. But there were others who said, 'You don't have to, we must not take that risk. What we must do is get these people to understand that it is disastrous for people to oppose white supremacy... our treatment must make them never again resist white supremacy. If you give them newspapers they are going to be aware of the support which they are enjoying both nationally and internationally'.

Some warders would leave newspapers behind in our cells deliberately. My first punishment was for possessing a newspaper which a warder left me.

If the regime wanted to persecute you, the easiest way was through the warders. But when you had a good relationship with the warders in your section it became difficult for the higher-ups to treat you roughly. In that way we were able to win the support of many warders.

Lieutenant Gregory, as his present rank is, was one of the most refined warders, well-informed and courteous with everybody, soft-spoken... a person with very good observation. I developed a lot of respect for him.

You are old or young depending on how you feel in your spirit... and you can put a lot of verve in you by the ideas that you hold. If you feel that you still have a role to play you will look relaxed and young, but if you think you have reached the end of your life then of course that must be reflected in your appearance, your demeanour or the way you walk.

The extent to which our ideas were supported by democrats both inside and outside the country was a source of tremendous inspiration, and it brought us happiness to know that the regime's efforts to isolate us and make us forgotten by people outside had completely failed.

I am grateful in some ways. Although Robben Island was a tragedy, we had the opportunity to stand back from ourselves and evaluate our work collectively and individually and the mistakes we had made. We all benefitted from that process.

But the memory of what happened there must be preserved. Robben Island should be developed as a museum where the people's history is preserved... a place for archives.. it is too important to be turned into a mere tourist resort.

James Gregory, Lieutenant in the Prison Department, was Nelson Mandela's personal warder for many years.

THE JAILER
James Gregory

I went to the Island in 1966 and left in 1976. For most of these ten years I was head of the censor department. Everything goes through that office — letters, applications for visits... it was a sort of lifeline for the prisoners. The censor had to read each letter and take out political things that were not allowed.

Robben Island's political prisoners had minds of their own and were more difficult than the ordinary commonlaw criminal. You got to know that if there was something they wanted, they would keep on and on until they got it.

When I went to the Island I was told that these people were terrorists... it was fed to you every day, in the media, radio, whatever... you thought you were going to find a lot of monsters there. I kept my distance in the beginning, but as time went on I realised these people were not that bad. Knowing the culture of the black, 'cos I grew up with them, I realised why these people were in prison... for the cause. I grew up in Zululand and my friends were black boys of my age... I had no white friends, so I learnt their culture, their ways, their language...

In the beginning of my time on the Island, if anything went wrong, if a letter didn't reach home or a letter from home didn't reach a prisoner, the censor's office was blamed and the prisoner would come on very aggressive. But the more they got to know me and I them, it became more amiable... we understood each other. I never lied to them... I might say, 'Look, I've got this letter, but I'm not going to give it to you for certain reasons, I'm putting it on your file'. So I would tell him and not hide it from him. Their trust in me grew because of that.

I spoke to some of them in Xhosa, or in Zulu, depending on how educated they were, but mostly we spoke English to each other. Some of their visitors could not speak English or Afrikaans. If the visitor said something that was not allowed I would tell them to leave the topic alone. I never had an argument from the prisoner. They knew that I was just doing the job. They also knew that any personal matters and troubles I heard were never repeated. Some of their girlfriends found other boyfriends and there were quite a few heated arguments.

The leadership group, there were eight of them, called themselves the government in exile, and they became my responsibility. I think my commissioner thought that I was the correct guy for the job. Later, when he left the Island, I was solely in charge of Mr Mandela. I got to know his family very well and I was trusted with things that even today people don't know about, and obviously I'll never betray that trust. We actually became friends. He always called me Mr Gregory, never by my rank. I would call him Mandela, or Nelson, and I asked him if he minded being called this. Since he's been out, he's phoned me a few times and he calls me James and I call him Mr Mandela. Mr Mandela is a perfect gentleman.

As Mandela became more important, more and more people wanted to come and see him... some out of curiosity, many trying to climb on the bandwagon. I was very much the buffer between him and the outside world. It got so bad that eventually I would ask him who he actually wanted to see. And there were family worries, little matters that he could not solve himself but which I could quite easily do. In that way I think I kept a lot of pressure off him.

To tell you the truth I had no idea then that he was likely to be President. It was only later, in 1985, that I started realising what was happening. A change had to come to majority rule, and I think the obvious man (for President) is Mr Mandela.

James Gregory was born on 7th November 1941. He came to Robben Island in 1966 and was put in charge of the censor department. He was later appointed Mandela's personal warder, serving in that capacity until 1990. He retired in April 1994.

PRISONER 467/64
Andrew Mlangeni

I had never been sentenced or been in prison, so the Rivonia Trial conviction and sentence was an experience for me. We were sentenced on 13th June 1964 in Pretoria and we had no idea where we'd be going'. When we enquired they said, 'Don't worry, you'll know by tomorrow where you'll be going. At 4 am the next day they came and woke us up... we were handcuffed and put into a truck. We arrived at an army camp in Pretoria where we were put into an army plane and flown to Robben Island. I didn't know anything about the Island except what I read in history books... I knew that it was somewhere in the Atlantic Ocean and somewhere near Cape Town.

We landed there at quarter to nine in the morning. It was a very cold day... we were then taken to isolation cells. Robben Island was a strange place. One of the things that struck me was the openness. Remember, we had been detained in Pretoria, surrounded by huge buildings. My first impression was that, even if I'm going to spend the rest of my life here, this is an open space and one is going to get fresh air... we'll see the ocean, the ships passing, the trees...

There were only a few cells at the beginning so we virtually built the prison ourselves. We had to produce the lime that was required, the bricks, the stones, to build more and more cells.

The Rivonia Trialists were separated from the rest of the prisoners because we were treated as leaders. We were isolated and put into single cells. A few days after our arrival we were taken out for the first time to work in the courtyard, little knowing that people from Britain would be arriving... I think they represented the *Daily Telegraph*. They found us knitting jerseys. The prison authorities said, 'This is the type of work we are giving them, not hard labour'. The moment they left, everything was taken away and stones and big rocks were brought into the yard on wheelbarrows. Our instructions were to break them into small stones. That was the type of work we did for a month. After this we worked in the lime quarry where former leaders such as Makana, Chief Cetewayo and Harry the Strandloper had worked. We worked under very harsh conditions — it was hot and the glare of the lime spoilt the eyes of many prisoners.

They opened up the cells at seven in the morning and we walked to the lime quarry... you had to produce a certain amount of lime every day... sometimes ten full wheelbarrows. If you did not meet the requirements you would be punished and the common punishment was to deprive you of food for three days. I worked on the lime quarry from 1964 to 1978. Warders behaved like animals, wild animals. You had to dig every minute until 12 o'clock... they stood at a distance watching... they would shout at you as if you were not a human being.

I think our wives were counselled by family and friends. They were told to show a brave face and pretend nothing was wrong, so that they did not demoralise the person in prison. That was also our attitude towards visitors... we must appear happy and not bothered by life in prison. I think my wife played her cards very well... I don't know if I played mine as well. I think women are strong... spiritually, physically... It is wrong to speak about women as the weaker sex. My wife singlehandedly brought up our children, despite continuous police harassment.

I got out of prison after 26 years and four months. To my surprise it didn't take me long to adjust... I adjusted quicker than my wife. I'm the happiest man. I've now been married 44 years and I challenge you young chaps to beat that.

Andrew Mlangeni was born on June 6th 1925. He was arrested on 11th July 1963 and charged with sabotage. He was convicted to life imprisonment at the Rivonia Trial and was sent to Robben Island on 14th June 1964. He was released in 1989 having spent a total of 26 years in prison. After the April 1994 elections, Mlangeni became a member of Parliament.

June Mlangeni, wife of Andrew Mlangeni, who brought up their four children on her own during the 26 years of Andrew's imprisonment.

THE WIFE
June Mlangeni

We were young when Andrew was arrested and I was looking forward to the future with him... but it was torn apart by a government which separated two people who aimed to build a future together. After I saw him on Robben Island I became stronger, and I could cope better with the police harassment. Before I used to shiver when the knock came at 2 am knocking from window to door, front and back doors... and they knew that I was a woman alone in the house. Dozens came — as though my house was a criminal house. I was harassed many times and my children were harassed.

When Andrew was arrested I was a housewife... I started to work when Andrew was in prison and I took time off to go to court to listen to Andrew's case... then my employers found out that my husband was one of the Rivonia Trialists, and I was fired.

It was difficult for the first ten years... being a mother of four young children... I wasn't working, I had to pay rent. But I knew why he was on the Island... because of his people, because of me, because of the children, because of his country.

When the permit came to visit Andrew, I borrowed money for a third class ticket to Cape Town. The train took two nights and I arrived at seven in the morning. I had to be at the docks at one, which was when the boat left. I walked from the station to the harbour, which is a long way, got onto the boat and arrived at Robben Island. There were a lot of police and I was escorted to a waiting room. I was then taken to see Andrew, who was standing at the end of a long passage. There were many other families and everyone was shouting at one another over the noise... sometimes I couldn't hear what he said. We were only given 30 minutes. He looked terrible, in short pants, a canvas jacket, with sandals... and the weather was cold. I didn't want to show him how hurt I was.

On my second visit I missed the boat. Our train was delayed because of an accident on the line and when I arrived at the docks the boat had already left. I roamed Cape Town's streets looking for help. I saw a church and met a priest who went with me to the docks to try and get an afternoon visit. They still refused. They could have listened, they could have seen that this person had come from far away and that it was not her fault that the train was late. But they did not want to listen.

We suffered greatly on these early visits to Robben Island. We often had no place to sleep, no place to change our clothes. When Cowley House opened in Cape Town it was a refuge for the family and friends of prisoners. I said to myself, 'God has heard our prayers'. You had a bed to sleep in, you had food to eat, you had a bath to yourself, so that you could prepare yourself for your visit to your husband on the Island.

We were examples for the younger wives — we told them that their visits must give courage to the prisoners, who mustn't feel that they are forgotten. We started to organise visits for those prisoners whose families did not come because of police harassment.

When Andrew was released and came home I didn't want to leave him alone for even a few minutes... I wanted to be with him all the time.

June Mlangeni was born on 22nd March 1928. She married Andrew in December 1949 and they had four children. 'It was difficult being a mother of four small children. I had to pay rent, and I was working. Two hands are better than one hand — one hand cannot wash without the other hand, so it was very difficult'. June Mlangeni is a member of the ANC PWV Women's League Committee.

PRISONER 471/64
Walter Sisulu

I was completely relaxed when I arrived on Robben Island although I knew how brutal and humiliating the treatment was to prisoners. We knew that the Island was no ordinary prison and that its main aim was to punish and demoralise. But we were very conscious of the legacy of Robben Island and the political leaders who had been imprisoned there... Makana, Maqoma, Harry the Strandloper. We were inspired by these great leaders.

One thing they did to demoralise you was to keep moving you from one cell to another for no particular reason. The other method was to discourage links with your family. At first you only received one letter in six months, and when you received them they were torn and scratched and you were left with a few lines saying the children are well. This was very painful. My son visited me once and after ten minutes they ended the visit because of something they thought he said.

One unhappy incident occurred on 29th May 1977 when they raided our cells at night. Many prisoners were beaten. They stripped me and told me to put my hands against the wall. I was worried because I had flu. I thought that their plan may be that I become ill and eventually die. I felt angry and bitter, it was one of the horrible invasions of our privacy. But, my position was better than a man like Toivo ja Toivo. He fought back after a beating and his cell was full of blood.

Mental torture was there all the time. At the lime quarry we tried to sing to gain morale, but when the authorities saw that this was building up our confidence they stopped us. I think we were the only prisoners in the country who were stopped from singing... but we still conversed and exchanged views. The quarry became the centre of the university of the Island. When we got to the quarry we took our spades and shovels and formed study groups.

Robben Island united us more than anything else could have done. We had already experienced unity in the Treason Trial, and on the Island we began to widen our horizons politically. We developed friendships despite our political differences and united in dealing with matters related to prison issues.

I missed civilised society outside very much, not only my family but people generally. They attempted to deprive us of information, and newspapers were not allowed at all. Not to have a newspaper was a punishment I cannot describe... I must have a newspaper, it's part of my life. And I missed children very much. You long for children more than anything else. You know, when children cry it makes you feel very unhappy — but it makes you happy just to hear the voice of a child.

The authorities knew that they had to deal with the leaders, and that Nelson was our spokesman. Because, rather than take orders, we discussed our plans and supervised each other. We cleaned our own cells and dishes because we wanted to see the prison tidy.

Shortly after our imprisonment, a rightwing paper from Britain came to the Island. A picture was taken of me talking to Nelson. We knew that it was going to be used for rightwing propaganda but we thought we should take advantage of the situation. In the picture we are discussing this very issue.

I had no problems when I came out — except for lights. I don't like darkness but my wife takes the opposite view. She switches the lights off and I switch them on, like the prisoner and the warder. In prison the light was on throughout the night and I got used to the lights.

Walter Sisulu, born on 18th May 1912, was arrested in July 1963 and charged with sabotage at the Rivonia Trial. He was sentenced to life imprisonment on 13th June 1964 and was sent to Robben Island on 14th June 1964. He was transferred to Pollsmoor Prison in April 1982 and released on 15th October 1989. He served a total of 25 years in prison, having spent 18 years of this on Robben Island. In April 1994, Walter Sisulu was Deputy President of the ANC.

PRISONER 21/67
Govan Mbeki

The warders on Robben Island did not regard us as normal human beings. I don't know if it would be correct to say that they even regarded us as animals because they cared a lot for their animals. I would say that they regarded us as a deadly enemy which had to be destroyed. If they were not going to destroy us physically then they wanted to destroy our thinking. They wanted to make us believe that we would never enjoy the democratic rights for which we had fought so long.

We, the Rivonia Group, were mentally but not physically abused. The psychological impact of the treatment, sometimes subtle, sometimes brazen, made us feel lower than the warders. When we arrived on the Island we would address the warders in Afrikaans as Meneer, which is Mister in English, but they wouldn't accept that. The warders would say, 'I'm not a kaffir Minister of Religion... you should call me boss, not Mister'. After many years they accepted our addressing them as Mister.

African prisoners were put on the F diet scale which meant mealie pap in the morning with a little bit of sugar, boiled mealies at lunch, and in the evening it was back to mealie pap, but without sugar. Three times a week we got some meat. The D diets were for the coloured and Indian prisoners. They also had mealie pap in the morning but with milk, sugar and a mug of coffee. And for lunch they had mealie rice with fat in it, and bread in the evening. This bread was given the name 'katkop', which means the head of the cat, and it was smeared with dripping. We had no bread. It was only in about 1975, eleven years after we'd been there, that bread was given to us, and even then it was one slice three times a week. We longed for bread... people who have never been denied bread can't imagine how we longed for bread. What struck us as strange was that the very people who denied us bread were very keen to tell us almost daily that they were religious Christians. They probably said prayers twice daily with their families, 'give us this day our daily bread', yet to them we were not part of the 'us' who should be given our daily bread.

In the early years you were allowed half an hour exercise in the morning and half an hour in the afternoon. You had nothing to read and no bed, just a mat. The winters can be terribly cold, and you'd sit in your cell on your mat wearing short pants, a canvas jacket and sandals with no socks. They often deliberately gave us tattered and dirty clothes which was calculated to demoralise us... but we would not go under.

The warders tried to drive us very hard. But we had been involved in the resistance struggle for so long that we were able to devise ways of limiting the amount of work. We kept the pace of work down by wielding the pick up and down in rhythm, which preserved our energy. If we found that someone working too fast we would say, 'the white man's work never gets finished, comrades'.

Sometimes we beat them at their own game, which made us feel jubilant. For example, communication between the sections was strictly prohibited, but we managed to get round this. It was pure joy when we made this breakthrough because we could now communicate with our comrades in ways which were not visible to the authorities. There's nothing like success, it makes one feel so nice.

One method of communication was through the kitchen. The kitchen was manned for a long time by common law criminals. We battled for a long time to get our own people into the kitchen. They smuggled notes to us by putting them

Govan Mbeki born on 8th July 1910, was arrested on 11th July 1963 and at the Rivonia Trial was found guilty of sabotage. He was given a life sentence and sent to Robben Island on 14th June 1964. He was released on 5th November 1987 having spent 23 years and five months on Robben Island. Soon after April 1994, Mbeki was elected Vice-President of the Senate.

at the bottom of the drums of boiled mealies. Sometimes we were caught out — once for example our notes floated to the top of a drum of soup.

Communication was essential for keeping up the morale of the prisoners as well as disseminating information from one section to another.

Nelson Mandela, Walter Sisulu, Raymond Mhlaba and myself were never allowed to be together in a group but we overcame this by consulting two at a time and ultimately we would arrive at a collective decision.

Each of our cell doors had a window with four panes. These were sealed so that you could not hear what was going on around you. However, the warders found this a problem because they couldn't communicate with us on their morning visits. So an order was given to open the top two panes. We were then able to communicate and our voices could be heard in the passage between the two rows of cells. Amazingly the acoustics were so good that one's voice travelled right down the passage.

We organised concerts for birthdays or for the end of the year, and we would stand at the windows and sing songs or recite poems. A range of music came through those windows, including *Blue River,... Be Mine*. You would clap your hands inside your cell and the sound would travel through the windows. Lectures were also given at these windows for all the people in the passage.

I had a guitar in prison. It was bought from money sent in by friends and relatives. One of my comrades, who was very good with his hands, made a casing for it out of scrap material collected on the island. I played the guitar quite a lot, at first with Neville Alexander and then with a group of other prisoners.

One occasionally got off the Island to see medical specialists at Cape Town Hospital. The moment you got to the mainland, leg-irons were strapped to your legs and you were pushed into a sealed van. When you got out of the van you were handcuffed and with these handcuffed hands you had to hold up the leg-irons. This was one of the most humiliating experiences. When you got to the outpatient department there was a general buzz, like a beehive, from the hundreds of outpatients. The moment a prisoner appeared in leg-irons and handcuffs, the people were suddenly quiet. You would feel their eyes penetrating your entire being. It was an experience one doesn't like to recall.

When a political prisoner goes to jail he says to himself, 'I am not going to allow myself to go under'. He devises ways to achieve this, and one way was through political and formal education. Some of our comrades entered jail illiterate. At the quarry we taught them to read and write. As there was no paper we used to write on the sand and on the lime. When we worked in groups at the lime quarry the lecturer of the group would do less physical work than his students. We put prisoners through all levels of primary and secondary school and even through to degree level. After a five year sentence these illiterate prisoners were able to read letters from their families and also to write letters. Eddie Daniels, who had a 15 year sentence, left Robben island with two degrees, something he could never have achieved outside prison.

Prisoners were regularly brought from Robben Island to Cape Town's Groote Schuur Hospital for treatment in the outpatient section. They shuffled along the passage in leg irons.

We became more and more conscious of the history of Robben Island, of the days of the Dutch East India Company when the Island was used for political

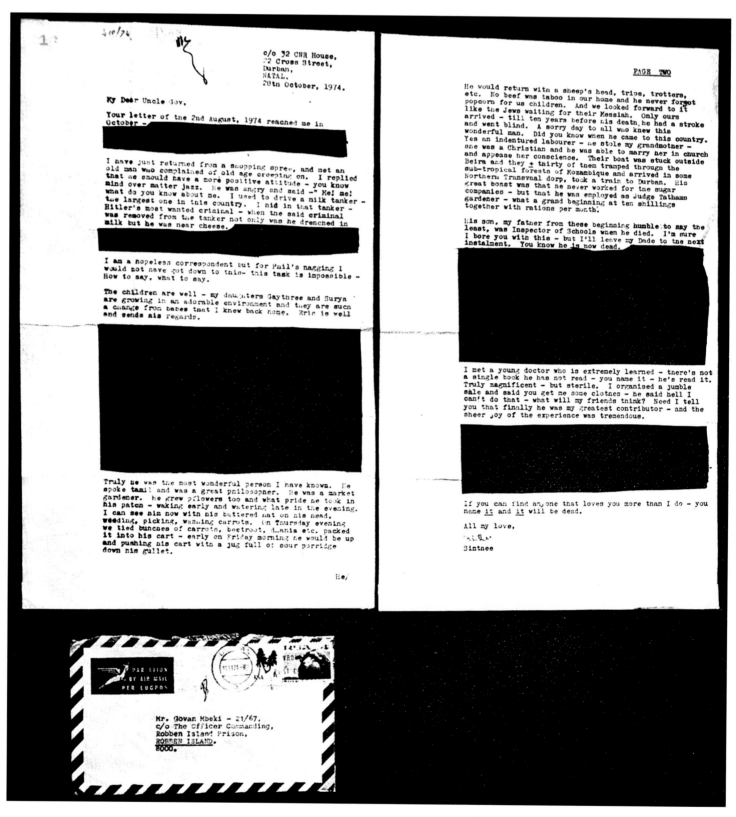

c/o 32 CNR House,
72 Cross Street,
Durban,
NATAL.
28th October, 1974.

My Dear Uncle Gov,

Your letter of the 2nd August, 1974 reached me in October – ████████████████████████████

I have just returned from a shopping spree, and met an old man who complained of old age creeping on. I replied that he should have a more positive attitude – you know mind over matter jazz. He was angry and said –" Me! me! what do you know about me. I used to drive a milk tanker – the largest one in this country. I hid in that tanker – Hitler's most wanted criminal – when the said criminal was removed from the tanker not only was he drenched in milk but he was near cheese. ████████████████

I am a hopeless correspondent but for Phil's nagging I would not have got down to this– this task is impossible – How to say, what to say.

The children are well – my daughters Gaythree and Surya are growing in an adorable environment and they are such a change from babes that I knew back home. Eric is well and sends his regards.

████████████████████████████████

Truly he was the most wonderful person I have known. He spoke tamil and was a great philosopher. He was a market gardener. He grew flowers too and what pride he took in his patch – waking early and watering late in the evening. I can see him now with his battered hat on his head, weeding, picking, washing carrots. On Thursday evening we tied bunches of carrots, beetroot, dhania etc. packed it into his cart – early on Friday morning he would be up and pushing his cart with a jug full of sour porridge down his gullet.

He/

He would return with a sheep's head, tripe, trotters, etc. No beef was taboo in our home and he never forgot popcorn for us children. And we looked forward to it like the Jews waiting for their Messiah. Only ours arrived – till ten years before his death, he had a stroke and went blind. A sorry day to all who knew this wonderful man. Did you know when he came to this country. Yes an indentured labourer – he stole my grandmother – she was a Christian and he was able to marry her in church and appease her conscience. Their boat was stuck outside Beira and they ± thirty of them tramped through the sub-tropical forests of Mozambique and arrived in some Northern Transvaal dorp, took a train to Durban. His great boast was that he never worked for the sugar companies – but that he was employed as Judge Tathams gardener – what a grand beginning at ten shillings together with rations per month.

His son, my father from these beginning humble to say the least, was Inspector of Schools when he died. I'm sure I bore you with this – but I'll leave my Dad to the next instalment. You know he is now dead.

████████████████████████████████

I met a young doctor who is extremely learned – there's not a single book he has not read – you name it – he's read it. Truly magnificent – but sterile. I organised a jumble sale and said you get me some clothes – he said hell I can't do that – what will my friends think? Need I tell you that finally he was my greatest contributor – and the sheer joy of the experience was tremendous.

████████████████████████████████

If you can find anyone that loves you more than I do – you name it and it will be dead.

All my love,

Sinthee

A censored letter to Uncle Gov, from Sinthee.

prisoners, as a leper institute and so on. We learnt about some of our generals who had been banished to the Island — Makana the left-handed, Langalibalele from Natal and Maqoma, who died on the Island in September 1873. There was also the time in 1978 when the Government used Maqoma's memory as a propaganda exercise. The then leader of the Ciskei bantustan, Lennox Sebe, visited the Island with some of his followers, to try and find Maqoma's remains. The prison authorities did not have a record of who was buried where, so they brought a witchdoctor to find the exact spot, but to us this seemed to be pure guesswork. When we walked past the cemetery and saw them digging we doubted that they were in fact exhuming the remains of Maqoma... but it satisfied them. The South African government wanted to humour Lennox Sebe by allowing him to re-inter Maqoma's remains on Mount Indoda in the Ciskei and make a shrine there. I suppose these are the building blocks of nationalism and the government encouraged that — they wanted the Ciskei people to look back on what Verwoerd called a 'dead past' and create an ethnic mythology. It suited the Apartheid system which encouraged small tribal groupings to be separate from one another. It suited their puppet system because by dividing them it was easier to control, exploit and oppress the African people.

We knew that no tyrant is there for all time and that however well armed he may be, the will of the people would overcome the tyrant's forces. We knew therefore that at some stage we would get out of jail and that we must prepare ourselves for that time. The Nationalists didn't learn the lesson that an organisation that leads people against oppression and racism cannot be destroyed.

Long before the compass was invented people used to sail the seas, and they were guided by the stars above them. We also had starts to guide us in the darkest moments of the struggle, but not the physical stars. Our stars were the basic policy issues that guide the African National Congress — the basic principles set out in the Freedom Charter. This meant that even if a man or woman was locked up in an isolation cell somewhere in the country with no contact with comrades, he or she was guided by the principles one was fighting for. Those were our guiding stars.

The day I was released I was assured by a major in charge of security that I was going to be released unconditionally. On the day of my release I was told to get my things together quickly and I was hurried to the landing strip on Robben Island. A helicopter took me to the military airport outside Cape Town and from there I was taken to Pollsmoor where I was allowed to see Nelson for an hour. Then I flew to Port Elizabeth. Because I had no address in Port Elizabeth, having left in the early 1960s, they allowed me to spend 48 hours at the Holiday Inn. As soon as I got there I was told that I would be addressing a press conference. I assumed it would be composed of representatives of the three local papers. I was met by a crowd of some 200 journalists and TV people with flashing lights that blinded me. It was an experience I will not easily forget and one that probably led to my being banned three weeks after my release from jail.

PRISONER 41/78
Tokyo Sexwale

I was sentenced to 18 long years on Robben Island. You must eventually like the place if you are to survive. I loved it because it was a place of fresh air, fresh ideas, fresh friendships, and teaching the enemy...We were all convicted, prisoner and jailer... we were chained to one another.

Many warders had strange ideas — that we were terrorists with horns, long tails, long nails, long teeth. It was a shock for them to enter Robben Island and find a Catholic prisoner who wanted to see his priest, to find a prisoner speaking Afrikaans, because they thought we only spoke Russian or Cuban, to find that they were dealing with educated, intellectual people. Eventually we were able to find common ground... and strong friendships were built.

When I arrived I was entrusted with the responsibility of collecting news. Imprisonment is harsh if you don't know what's happening outside. We knew about the ANC attack on the South African Air Force Headquarters through one of the warders who excitedly gave us that morning's paper. The news of the Nkomati Accord also came via a warder who mentioned this in order to demoralise us. We learned of the Silverton Siege from a newspaper given to us by a common law prisoner. It was important for us to know the level of resistance in the country, what was happening in all the Frontline States, the balance of forces between the East and West and the general anti-Apartheid struggle in the world.

The other critical thing was political education. I had to translate ANC policies so that everyone could understand them. We transformed Robben Island into a university of the ANC. We saw ourselves as revolutionaries, and we lived according to a strict code of conduct. Things like pin-up pictures were not acceptable. We remembered important dates like the birth of the ANC, Africa Day, May Day, the formation of Umkhonto we Sizwe, Heroes Day, 16th June 1976 and the birth of the Communist Party. We would hold little rallies in the different sections and have discussions, poetry reading and plays.

To survive on Robben Island your mind must travel far and you must keep physically fit. Sport was critical in keeping body and soul together and diffusing frustration. We even tried to introduce golf, but the authorities refused, saying that the balls would fall into the ocean and if you went to collect them you might not come back.

I also learnt to play the classical guitar. The authorities did not realise that in allowing us these instruments they were giving us another avenue to conduct our struggle. We sang songs against the government and against Apartheid... we sang songs in praise of our heroes, and our policies... and of course we sang love songs. We had 6000 records, from Satchmo and Jim Reeves to Michael Jackson. Each section could select music for one week. This music was played in the morning, during lunch and in the evening. This was before television and videos.

Many improvements on Robben Island came through struggle. Some struggles involved deputations to magistrates, parliamentarians, Ministers, and the Red Cross, as well as go-slows. If these failed we went for hard methods such as hunger strikes. But the main lifeline for a political prisoner was his family who could pass messages on to pressure groups outside. Legal firms were held in very high esteem, and para-legals such as Judy were really critical.

You're often not prepared for a relationship to develop. You meet a person and appreciate them, and after a while you see beyond those qualities. Judy and I fell in love. We could only sit and talk when she managed to come to Robben Island on her own. It was an eye-opener for the warders, all white, all male, 99% Afrikaner — here was a white woman falling in love with, in their view, someone unacceptable, a terrorist, a Communist. But as we, as prisoners, became acceptable to them as leaders, they began to accept my relationship with Judy.

Our love was born out of the very stringent, harsh conditions of my imprisonment on Robben Island, an Apartheid prison. She's white and young, I'm black and quite young. I'm fierce looking, according to government descriptions, she's a tiny young woman. It was a difficult relationship in those conditions, but we braved it and decided to defend the simple, humble feelings that start between two people.

Space was denied us on Robben Island. Space was one of the things I was dying for. My cell was so small I didn't even have enough room to stretch my legs. In our house I don't like small things like coffee tables, they're just in the way.

Tokyo Sexwale born on the 5th March 1953. He was arrested in 1977 and in 1978 was sentenced to 18 years on Robben Island for sabotage. He was released in 1990. Tokyo Sexwale spent 13 years on Robben Island. After the April 1994 elections Sexwale was elected Premier of the PWV Province.

Judy Moon, who married Tokyo Sexwale after his release from Robben Island.

LEGAL ASSISTANT
Judy Moon

I was working for the human rights department at a firm of attorneys in Cape Town, doing mostly detainee work. In 1985 I started working with lawyers who dealt with about 40 clients on Robben Island. It was very impersonal at that stage — a prisoner would write to us with a query and we'd write back. Then one of the lawyers said, 'why don't you come and visit with us?' I finally met these faceless people. And I realised that they really needed someone to take an interest in them. I found that they were wonderful people, warm, loving and open.

The political prisoners were very disciplined and well educated — very different from the common law prisoners. The warder gave me a good example of the difference — if they left a R5 note and a newspaper in their office, they would never worry about the money with a political prisoner, just the newspaper. The discipline was unbelievable — there was no dagga-smoking, no smuggling of liquor — they could never be bribed in that way. It was often a little irritating —

we'd suggest something and it would take weeks to get an answer, because the whole prison, all 365 prisoners, had to be consulted. So my work became more like social work. If prisoners didn't receive letters, they wanted to know why, and I would be the person who would find their families. Of course there were problems. There was a quota system of letters and visits, but I did everything I could to let them have more outside contacts.

The prisoners became quite demanding the more I worked with them and I had to be very careful not to have favourites. Some of them didn't believe that I was the Judy Moon who had written to them. They'd say, 'We imagined you to be this huge fat woman,'... I'd say 'Why?' and they'd say, 'Because you work hard and you achieve a lot so you must be big, but actually you're small'. I think they were also surprised that a white person was so willing to help.

When I first started working on Robben Island the prisoners were not allowed to receive anything, not even a block of chocolate. So we smuggled a few blocks of chocolate in the files we brought to meetings. As time went on we became very friendly with the warders. They allowed the prisoners to eat with us, so I would pack sandwiches, chips, sweets and cooldrinks. It then became legal to take food so we made individual parcels of anything that would be a tasty treat.

When we could we smuggled letters because of the quota — prisoners who had been in prison for one or two years could receive and write only one or two letters a month. This included legal letters. It was essential that they had more communication. We became adept at smuggling letters — we'd put them in our bags and the prisoner would lean down and slip the letters into their shoes. We also fought to have privileged visits, as these did not come off their quota.

While I was working there about five prisoners asked to get married. Some were to women they had met while in prison, women who had started to correspond with them and then visited them, and others who had been sweethearts before they were sent to prison. Once special permission was granted we organised the wedding. The prisoner had to come to the mainland to Pollsmoor prison for the ceremony with one or two witnesses. We would hire or buy the prisoner his outfit, buy the rings, organise the photographs and get outfits for the bride and the parents. We would order a cake and put on a reception party at Pollsmoor with parents and warders. After cutting the cake the prisoner and his wife would each take half. Most prisoners wanted to keep their halves until they came out of prison, when they could share it with their bride. It was very sad actually, because for the half hour of the wedding the couple was never left alone, so they were not married in the true sense of the word... but it was also a happy time because it was exciting for them and meant an extra contact.

Tokyo was a very impressive and powerful person. I could see that he was in command of himself and knew how to survive in prison. He was chairperson of the recreation committee and it was through this that we got to know each other, as I organised all the videos. We both realised that our feelings were becoming stronger and we tried to get as many visits as possible. I was quite scared to allow my feelings to develop because I didn't know what was going to happen when he was released. But you can't help your feelings and it didn't matter to me that he still had so many years to serve. I think it would be difficult for me to understand Tokyo if I hadn't worked with him on Robben Island.

Judy Moon was born on 25th May 1960. She met Tokyo when she visited Robben Island on a regular basis in her capacity as assistant in a legal firm. Judy Moon and Tokyo Sexwale were married on 11th February 1993, and since Sexwale's appointment as Premier of the PWV, Judy acts as first Lady of the PWV Province.

PRISONER 350/64
Steve Tshwete

Robben Island was a real struggle for survival against assault and insult, with warders shouting, 'You will never get your freedom... you are nothing, just a kaffir. The white man is here to rule and this is his country... you are here to serve the white people of this country. A kaffir is a dog and you are a dog, and Mandela is a dog. You can have 101 doctorates but you are a kaffir... you are a number... you are nothing'.

Strip searches, which the warders enjoyed, were a means of humiliating you. When we came back from the quarry we had to queue up. Everyone had to take off their clothes to be searched. On cold days this was prolonged and some people would collapse. If this happened, the next morning you would have to go to hospital. That was a nightmare. You stood there naked in a queue waiting for the doctor. When you eventually saw him he usually wasn't interested. Some doctors were even drunk. One old man was very ill and we took him to hospital in a blanket. The warder in charge, who had a terrible reputation for killing prisoners, said, 'What is wrong with this thing?' and he then sjamboked him.

There were also strip searches at night and you had to stand naked facing the wall for many hours. During one of these searches the warders queried an educational certificate belonging to one of the inmates. He had to explain what a certificate actually was. It was the first time this warder had seen a certificate. That was the type of warder we had on the Island, guys drawn from the *platteland* who had low educational levels. We embarked on numerous hunger strikes and court actions against the Department of Prisons to challenge the assaults and the treatment.

As part of our studies we read a lot about Nazi Germany and the concentration camps. We were convinced that we were in the hands of Hitler's heirs. There was one huge warder we called 'The diesel man'. During his inspections he would call you, 'Kaffir, Cannibal, Murderer'. When he moved away we would retort, 'You Nazi, go back to Germany, you are wanted for war crimes'.

Some warders, however, began listening when we said, 'You are South African like I am and both of us have a responsibility to build a free and democratic society for all... this is your home, this is my home... and I'm not inferior because I'm black, nor are you superior because you're white'. It began to dawn on them that we might be saying something relevant.

Sport was very important on the Island. It relieved the tension and anxiety about family, about home and about survival in prison itself. Rugby was organised on political lines, unlike soccer, which brought about a spirit of non-political togetherness amongst the inmates, with a common struggle for survival. I was on the executive committee of a number of soccer clubs and delegate to the Makana Football Association, which was an umbrella body for all the clubs.

Apart from sport we also organised choral groups, musical combos, a film club, a reading society and ballroom dancing groups. The guys who were involved in ballroom dancing before prison taught us the waltz, the foxtrot, the quickstep and so on and there would be competitions in the cells. We brightened up the cell with this sort of activity and an outstanding performance by a pair of dancers would be recognised by, not a clap, but a brush, one hand brushing against another. A clap would have attracted the warders' attention and entertainment was not allowed. We also had a number of comedians and storytellers on the Island who sometimes entertained us while we were chopping stones.

Steve Tshwete was born on 12th November 1938. He was arrested in 1963 and convicted of sabotage and furthering the aims of a banned organisation. On 14th February 1964 he was sentenced to 15 years on Robben island. He was released on 8th December 1976 having spent 12 years on Robben Island. After the April 1994 elections he was appointed Minister of Sport and Recreation in the new Cabinet.

PRISONER 468/64
Ahmed Kathrada

We arrived on Robben Island on the morning of 14th June 1964. We were the first prisoners to be flown direct to the Island. It was a bitterly cold, windy, rainy day. We were housed in the old prison because our prison was not yet complete.

My main recollection of that first morning related to the workings of Apartheid. I was the youngest of the Rivonia Group and I was also the only Indian. All my co-prisoners were my seniors in age and politics and they were all Africans. The first thing we had to do was to get into Robben Island clothing. I was given long pants, a jersey, shirt, jacket, shoes and socks. My fellow prisoners, such as Mbeki, who is 20 years my senior, Sisulu, who is about 18 years my senior, and Mandela, about 12 years my senior, were given the same clothing, except they were given short pants and no socks. As a special concession they were given shoes — according to regulations African prisoners were only allowed to wear sandals, which are normally made from tyres.

And there was discrimination in food. Coloured and Indian prisoners were given a different diet to Africans. I was given porridge, soup and coffee in the morning but the Africans were given less sugar. In the afternoon we were given mealie rice and African prisoners were given boiled mealies. In the evening we were given a quarter of a loaf of bread with thick margarine, a cup of soup and coffee and the African prisoners were given just porridge and soup — no coffee and no bread.

Right from the word go we had decided not to accept any indignities and humiliation, but also to abide by the regulations, as long as they did not infringe on our dignity. Instinctively we protested against the discrimination in clothing and food with hunger strikes, boycotts and representations. Within three years we managed to equalise prison clothing. Food took much longer.

In prison one's life was governed by regulations. It was Tolstoy who said that in prison the warders have regulations instead of hearts. Political prisoners were classified as D group prisoners which meant minimum privileges. We were allowed one visit every six months, we were not allowed to sing, we were not allowed to whistle, we were not allowed to treat warders with disrespect, we were not allowed to mix with prisoners from the other sections.

We were housed in a section called B Section which used to be called the Segregation Isolation Section. We were not allowed to communicate with any other prisoners, especially the political prisoners. They brought in about three common law prisoners to spy on us and, as they said, to teach us how to work. This strategy failed and the prisoners were removed. But we did manage to recruit one of these spies into our organisation and he is now an important man in the security department.

We had to establish our own methods of communication and we were often guilty of the so-called offense of 'abusing study privileges' — this meant that you had used paper for purposes other than studying. We used to write a lot of documents and news on toilet paper. When they caught us the punishment was to reduce the amount of toilet paper. They had Mr Mbeki counting eight leaves of toilet paper for each prisoner in the morning and eight in the afternoon.

Right from the start we organised ourselves politically for the purpose of discipline, continuing our political education and encouraging academic education. News was only allowed in 1980 so we had to try all sorts of methods

Ahmed Kathrada was born on 21st August 1929. He was charged with sabotage in the Rivonia Trial and was given a life sentence. He was sent to Robben Island in June 1964 where he was incarcerated until 21st November 1982. He was then sent to Pollsmoor Prison in October 1982 and was released from there in October 1989. He spent a total of 27 years and three months in prison, 18 years of which was spent on Robben Island. After the April 1994 elections Kathrada was appointed Political Advisor to the President.

to get news — stealing, bribing, blackmailing and begging. We were fairly successful and well informed. Whenever big events occurred outside the authorities reacted very severely against us and we would immediately guess that something good had happened outside. But, after the Soweto uprising they acted as though nothing had happened and we only learnt about it two months later when new prisoners came to the Island.

Japh Masemola was a genius with his hands. He made musical instruments, tools, and a masterkey which could open any door in the prison. We used the key to open up some of the empty cells in our section in order to store newspapers and literature. Once we buried a very significant document in the prison garden. It was Mr Mandela's autobiography. But we were caught and the three of us, myself, Sisulu and Mandela were punished — we lost our study privileges for several years.

The average warder could not understand our obsession with news. They bought newspapers mainly for the sports pages and would ignore the rest. Most warders came from relatively uneducated backgrounds and they often believed we came from very wealthy backgrounds. This added to their inferiority complex. They went out of their way to tell us how wealthy they were and that they owned farms. In reality they usually joined the prison service to escape military service. They were also reluctant to identify their Dutch ancestry and tried to convince us that they had French, not Afrikaans, backgrounds. Also, they could not stand the thought of prisoners, especially black prisoners, being more educated than them. The warders did try to study and many of them registered, but 90% dropped out. There was one amusing incident of a warder who went on holiday for six weeks, and when he returned said he had done two MA degrees.

Right from the beginning the authorities made it clear that their mission was to break our morale and to crush whatever political ideas we had. They inflicted all sorts of cruelties and humiliations on us and tried to bribe individuals into working for them. They failed in all this, and the goodness in the prisoners came to the surface. Try as they might they could not break our morale or change our ideas — we stood together as a united force against the authorities.

On the whole, prison was a very enriching experience and it would be wrong to portray the prison years as all negative. I have often referred to two little quotations — one about two prisoners looking out of a prison cell, and the one saw stars and the other saw bars... and the other quotation, from Oscar Wilde, 'Prison deeds like prison weeds, grows well in prison air... it is only what is good in man that wastes and withers there'. Prisoners felt differently towards deprivations — some felt that food was the main deprivation, others felt that it was the lack of contact with their families. The biggest deprivation for me was the lack of children. We were living in an unreal world without women and children. One wants to hear the laughter of children. Despite all these deprivations the political prisoners emerged on top and their morale was high.

When I came out of prison so many things were new to me. The first thing I came across was a cordless telephone. Another thing was this Gillette razor, and I just couldn't insert this type of blade into a razor. I also couldn't get used to handling money, since we didn't handle it in prison. Each time I have to pay for something now I'd rather pay with a note instead of having to count coins.

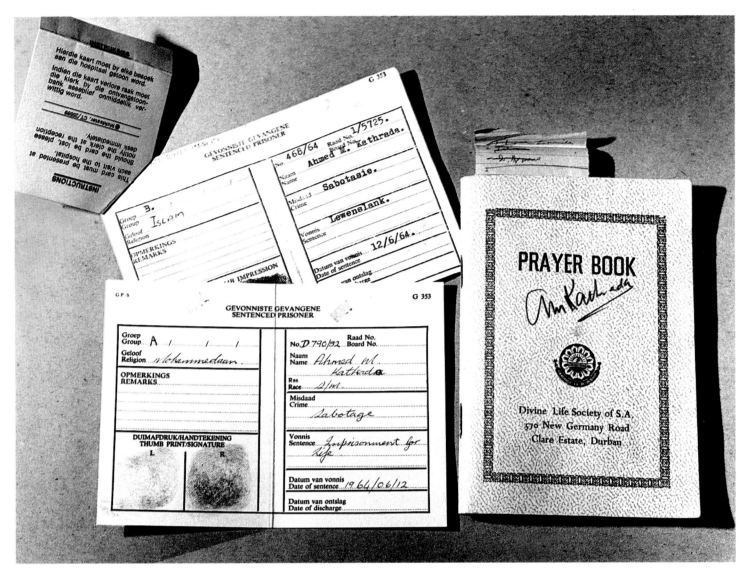

Ahmed Kathrada's Prayer Book and his
prisoner's document.

PRISONER 14/76
Patrick 'Terror' Lekota

It inspired us to know that we on Robben Island were following in the footsteps of a number of very noble characters who had stood up for the dignity and freedom of their people. The Island gave us a golden opportunity to develop a single national perspective by exchanging views with senior freedom fighters from all parts of the country.

We could not have anticipated all the pressures on the Island — such as being deprived of one's children. There would be the sudden anxiety that one could die on Robben Island without ever being able to make contact with one's child... or there was the possibility that something could happen to one's family. These kinds of pressures and tensions induced physical and mental breakdowns. One of the younger prisoners, who had had no legal representation, got a 40-year sentence, and it took him years before he grasped the reality of the situation — and he lost his mind.

In 1981 we mounted a six-day hunger strike which took place shortly after the Irish hunger strike in which Bobby Sands died. Over the years we had demanded the right to see our children, but the prison authorities argued that our children would be badly affected by visiting us terrorists. Our constant argument, however, was that while it was true that white society saw us as terrorists, we were regarded as heroes in our own community, and fighters for the freedom of our people. Our hunger strike eventually led to the amendment of the Prisons Act, and in 1982 children between the ages of three and 16 could come and visit us on Robben Island.

One of our concerns was whether our children would grow up to understand why we had chosen a life of prison instead of staying with them at home. We knew that what was being taught in the Bantu Education schools misinterpreted history, and that this might lead to our children rejecting us. I recalled that Nehru, while in jail, wrote to his daughter, explaining what he was fighting for. She later became Prime Minister of India. This inspired me to write a letter to my daughter explaining why I was in prison, and that the story of my arrest goes back to the year 1450 and the occupation of our land by the settlers.

The warders were primed to see us as terrorists, Communists and devils with horns. But these largely uneducated people, many of whom came from orphanages, eventually wanted to understand why we were there. It was tremendously refreshing and inspiring to see these ordinary people appreciating our cause. This experience led to my belief that South Africa had a promising future.

My nickname 'Terror'? Well, that came from being a striker in soccer. Many people thought that my name was given to me because I was a terrorist, but no, I was rather a terror for the goalkeepers of the opposition.

'Terror' Lekota was born on 13th August 1948. He was arrested in 1974 and charged with 'conspiracy to commit acts capable of endangering the maintenance of law and order'. The trial lasted 17 months and he spent six years on Robben Island and was released in December 1982. Lekota was detained in April 1985, and in June he and 21 others were charged with treason. In November 1986 Lekota was convicted of treason and sentenced to 12 years. He appealed, and in December 1989 the Appeal Court quashed all convictions. After the April 1994 elections Lekota was elected Premier of the Free State Province.

THE JAILER
Aubrey du Toit

When I arrived on the Island in 1976 my first impression was that it was a very solitary place. My colleagues told me that it wasn't a nice place to work, especially for a single man. You could only get off the Island every second weekend.

I enjoyed being close to the sea but it was quite hard to accept that you were so far from Cape Town. I enjoyed the village — it was like a big family. You had your ups and downs and your confrontations but you were forced to sort it out. You can't have enemies on a small island.

Before I was transferred I was told to treat the 'Pocos' differently and that I should keep my eyes and ears open and my mouth shut. When I grew up I had no contact whatsoever with black people, although I knew the so-called coloured people. It was a shock to meet these people (blacks) and see that they were intelligent human beings. As an Afrikaner I grew up believing that the ANC, PAC, Umkhonto we Sizwe meant the Communist enemy... your hair stood on end when you heard the name Nelson Mandela. These are the people who were going to take over our country. The Afrikaner people were frightened of them.

I was in charge of all prisoners' studies and was the local secretary for the University of South Africa. When a prisoner arrived on Robben Island I had to interview him and give him the different study options. Mr Nelson Mandela was very strict about people studying, not only prisoners but also warders. One day he asked me whether I was a student at UNISA. I said yes, and described my subjects, including one called Praktiese Afrikaans. He then said, 'Sergeant, you should be ashamed of yourself. I am Xhosa and I did Afrikaans and Nederlands... you are an Afrikaner and you did Praktiese (Practical) Afrikaans'.

My duties included censoring the study material and films as well as the outgoing assignments. I had no official training for this and sometimes I didn't know what I was looking for. For instance you as a warder knew nothing about political science, and yet you had to censor political science assignments. I remember I had to censor Andrew Mlangeni's assignments. He was an honours student in political science. Looking back I think it was a joke for an Afrikaner with Standard 10 to censor these difficult assignments.

Every Saturday there was a film and it was my job to censor that film — and once again I didn't know what to look for. I remember one film, *Judgement at Nuremberg* — I saw that in South Africa you could eventually have the same sort of judgements and I realised it was quite stupid to let that through.

Mr Mandela was a prisoner but also a leader, anybody could see that, even though he had no official status. The moment he walked into a room, his manner, his way of speaking, his dress, you knew he was a leader.

I regarded the prisoners as my friends, and I hope they saw me as a friend. I became more and more interested in their views and although I wasn't allowed to talk about politics we did have political discussions. It was a real eye-opener for me to see that they also wanted the best for South Africa.

Not long ago I was at Jan Smuts airport and I ran into what they call an ex-graduate from Robben Island and he greeted me very joyfully. We had a long discussion and I asked him how Mr Mandela was keeping, and he said fine.

Aubrey du Toit was born on 30th December 1957. He came to Robben Island in January 1976 to run the Prisoners' Studies Department. He handled the affairs of the leader's section and left Robben Island in November 1982. In 1994 Du Toit was an administrative assistant in an insurance company.

PRISONER 122/66

Kwedi Mkalipi

I was sentenced to 20 years on Robben Island and spent most of those 20 years there. I feel bitter about it. At one time I actually lost hope of ever coming out alive. They tried to dehumanise us. For a long time we were not allowed newspapers or books, except the Bible, and we were not allowed contact with people outside our section.

I have a sad story about the psychological torture we endured. I was very attached to my sister who was about to visit me. One day I was called into the office and a warder told me coldly that my sister was dead. I was stunned and could not believe what I was hearing. I said, 'What do you mean?' He said, 'I've told you that she's dead. What more do you want from me? You are wasting my time'. I said, 'But how did she die?' He replied, 'I don't stay with the kaffirs in Transkei — those are the people who will know how your sister died. Get out of my office'. When I got to my cell I cried for the first time since my imprisonment. This was cruelty in its worst form and I swore that I would never forgive these people for what they had done.

I remember another occasion when a priest was about to administer Holy Communion to us. A warder appeared and grabbed the bottle of wine that the priest was about to use. The warder said, 'Why give them wine? Why not water?' I was terribly shocked by this action, having grown up in a Christian environment. The priest then read a particular chapter from the Bible which saved my faith in Christianity. It was a letter from St Paul to the Ephesians: 'Put on the whole armoury of God that we may be able to stand against the wiles of the Devil... for we wrestle not against flesh and blood but against powers, against the rulers of darkness of this world, against spiritual wickedness in high places'. I saw how hurt this priest was and that he, a white man, was being ill-treated by another white man. I interpreted the 'spiritual wickedness' as the government from which I was expected to protect myself with the 'whole armoury of God'.

But the warders genuinely believed that black people were far inferior to them. One example was when one of our outstanding lawyers was writing a law exam and the prison official in charge of the studies said, 'It must be nice to be a Bantu because your papers are easier than the one the whites write'.

I belonged to the Pan Africanist Congress, and at the beginning there was hostility between the political groups. I remember a Brigadier engineered some of the hostilities. For example he would take a pick-axe and handle and put them to one side, saying sometime later that these were the weapons the PAC were going to use against the ANC. When we realised what was happening we refused to let the enemy capitalise on our political divisions.

There was also a lot of victimisation on the Island. Once they found a piece of paper in my pocket — a *Reader's Digest* article about Hiroshima. I was charged with possession of an unauthorised article. On the way to court they saw that I was wearing sunglasses, and I was charged again for possession of an unauthorised article. For both cases I was put on a spare diet; for three days you get the juice of the mealie rice; on the fourth day you'd be given cooked mealies and for the following three days the mealie rice liquid again; after that you would get half rations for a further 14 days.

When I left the Island after 20 years, I felt guilty about leaving my friends behind. I had cultivated strong relationships, the type of bonds that meant that whenever somebody got hurt by the warders we'd rush over and comfort them.

Kwedi Mkalipi was born on 21st March 1936. He was arrested in 1964 on a sabotage charge and was sent to Robben Island in 1966. He was released on 10th February 1985 having served 20 years on Robben Island. In 1994 Kwedi Mkalipi was working as a manager in a credit company.

PRISONER 363/64
Neville Alexander

All of us came to the Island with very different backgrounds. Our group had a very strong left-wing political background. Most of us had at least five years experience in student politics and in my own case experience also in what I'd call adult politics. We were aware that revolutionary activity could lead to imprisonment and this was very important from a psychological point of view — we were prepared for imprisonment. Having come from a Roman Catholic background with an exceptionally disciplined father, I think I was a model prisoner. It was no problem for me to follow rules, as long as they were humane. But if things became irrational then my radical and rebellious nature would just not accept any of this nonsense. Finally, people like Nelson Mandela and Walter Sisulu made us understand. They said, 'Look chaps, we're going to be here for quite a while... you're going to kill yourselves if you keep knocking against the granite wall'.

The experience of the Island was struggle in the most literal sense of the word because you had to struggle at all levels. First you had to struggle against the obvious representatives of the state, the white warders. It was a struggle for dignity even more than for survival, a dignity which is inherent in us as human beings, as people who had a sense of moral purpose in struggling for liberation. Then there was the other level which for me was the most important one — the struggle to know yourself.

The system was not only cruel to us but also to the warders. The innermost components of their own identity were challenged daily. They saw that we were scholars, disciplined and articulate, and these things obviously undermined the images they they had in their heads about us. Eventually we ended up teaching them subjects like History, Maths, English and even Afrikaans. We became very influential and that is why the prison authorities adopted a policy of rotating warders. Education made it possible for us to survive whole. We set up a schooling system and essentially turned the Island into an informal university.

Helen Suzman's visit to the Island in 1967 was one of the benchmarks of our imprisonment. She managed to get the authorities to allow her visit, and her perseverance demonstrated her commitment to human rights. After her visit we were allowed more visits and letters and it was easier to get permission to study.

Culturally the Island was quite a new experience. Most of the people in my group had a very European orientation and were well versed in European culture. It was the first time that we came together with people from a very African background. We learnt Xhosa and Sotho songs and learned about the pre-literate history of African groups. In the 1970s we were able to stage concerts over the Christian holidays with play readings and poetry readings. For me the highlights were the humorous moments. One of the nicest stories was one about Walter Sisulu who would always ask Joe Gqabe to sing a particular song called *Fatima My Love.* Joe would deliberately misunderstand and sing another, rather vulgar, song and Walter would always get very irritated. And you'd get someone like Nelson getting up and telling a story in English in a very wooden way, and the moment he switched to Xhosa it was quite different.

You also realised the importance of all those things you took for granted, such as your family, your circle of friends, your relationship with your parents. For all of us the greatest deprivation was not the sexual one but the separation from children. The fact that I never saw a child for ten years boggles my mind.

Neville Alexander was born on 22nd October 1936. He was arrested on 12th July 1963 on a charge of conspiring to commit sabotage. He was sent to the Island on 15th April 1964 and released on 13th April 1974, having served ten years in prison. In 1994, Alexander was the Director of the Alternative Education Project at the University of Cape Town.

PRISONER 864/64
Eddie Daniels

I went to the Island on 16th November 1964. I was sentenced to 15 years imprisonment for committing sabotage. I committed sabotage because I found the policies of Apartheid to be brutal, cruel and evil. I belonged to the African Resistance Movement and we attacked electric pylons and government installations.

I was also a member of the Liberal Party and had been part of a group which collected affidavits from short term prisoners on the Island after the 1960 Sharpeville incident. The stories they told me were absolutely frightening. One case involved Johnson Mlambo. He was forced to dig a hole, was put in that hole and the warders then urinated on top of him. The prisoners also told of warders who would single you out and humiliate you if you were educated. Dennis Brutus was so persecuted that he became mentally ill. The Liberal Party was the only organisation that published critical articles about Robben Island, calling it 'Devil's Island', and this created an international uproar.

My fellow accused were all whites and were sent to Pretoria prison. Because I was classified coloured I was sent to Robben Island. My isolation cell was like a death chamber, totally silent and everything around me was grey, cold, bleak and frightening. At first I could not eat the prison food because it stank, but after two weeks I started to eat just to survive.

But many of my fellow prisoners went out of their way to accommodate me. I remember the first day I was allowed out of my cell. As I walked to the bathroom my way was blocked by a very big, impressive person. I looked up and was utterly thrilled when I saw Nelson Mandela, who offered me his hand and said welcome. This helped break the ice. But I was still lonely for the first three years.

Nelson Mandela's influence on the island was tremendous — this man was so humble and yet so dynamic. Walter Sisulu was just as big a giant. When I felt demoralised I could hug them and their strength would flow into me. Many people came to Nelson and Walter from different political organisations to talk about their problems. Nelson and Walter showed us what it means to survive in the face of adversity, the meaning of true discipline.

Nelson Mandela was a good friend to me on the Island. Once when I was ill and was unable to get up to empty my chamberpot, Nelson Mandela came into my cell, asked me how I was and said, 'You just relax', and he took the chamberpot, emptied and cleaned it and brought it back. This was a really magnanimous gesture. It's a moment I will never forget.

I lived for escape. I tried to escape while in detention and when I was awaiting trial. Once we planned to leave the Island on a huge log, but security was too tight. Then I thought of organising an escape via helicopter. This escape had to take place from the mainland and could only be put into operation after my release. The idea was to rescue Nelson and Walter, who would be flown to the mainland to the grounds of an Embassy where they could ask for political asylum. The escape date was to be New Years Day 1981. But a condition of the ANC High Command on the Island was that the external wing must be part of the escape. Unfortunately I did not manage to get the plan to Mr Tambo in London, so although I spent three years planning the escape it did not actually come to fruition.

Eddie Daniels was born on 25th October 1928. He was sent to Robben Island on 17th November 1964 having been charged with sabotage. He was released on 16th November 1979 after having spent a total of 15 years on Robben Island. Daniels spent many years teaching and is now retired.

THE PRISONER 90/65
Satyandranath 'Mac' Maharaj

One of the things about recalling prison life is that you unconsciously black out the worst events and try to distill from your experience something that can give meaning to life. It was very important for us, as political people, to keep alive that spirit of resistance. When I try and look deeper I see how we had to interact with each other to build up a community feeling. Even now when I meet a fellow prisoner whom I haven't seen for many years there is a type of warmth which is connected to this deep common experience. We are building a New South Africa and we need to remember not only our resistance but our experience in building a community.

You had to see the white warders as individuals and learn to interact with them, if only to further your own purpose. You began to understand that because of their white skin the warders themselves were trapped by an outlook shaped by the system. One warder we struck up a relationship with was a fairly old Afrikaner. Through him we obtained a continuous supply of newspapers. On an initial assessment, one would have thought that a younger warder might be more receptive to smuggling news for us. But this old man was nearing retirement and was a member of the Jehovah's Church, so he had a certain pacifist streak.

When we eventually managed to get a regular supply of papers it became necessary to delay the dissemination of this news to avoid alerting the authorities. We devised an elaborate system in which I would get the newspapers at 8 pm every night and translate and transcribe them till 11 pm, when the warders changed shift and the papers had to be returned. The next day this set of translated news was given to another colleague to transcribe in his own handwriting, so that if anything went wrong it could not be traced to me. The news was then stored for three days and only then was it delivered to the prisoners. I must pay credit to our leadership here — for example news was like food to Comrade Sisulu — who resisted the temptation of coming to me for advance news.

From the day of my arrest I never gave up the idea of escaping. However, escape meant working with great determination and steadfastness, continuously accumulating tools and instruments that might be useful. For example, you might come across a piece of flat steel which had no immediate use but, if stored, might come in useful. This happened when we made the master key for Robben Island from some steel we found. Jafta Masemola of the PAC was recruited to help. He and I took some lard and filed down that piece of iron so that it fitted the lock in my cell. We then had to ensure it fitted all locks as well as the gates to the external entrances. The key, which was made on the Easter Weekend of 1971, was used very productively and it gave us access to empty cells where we could store our communication material. I also hoped that the key could be used for escape purposes.

One escape plan which went the furthest was when Nelson Mandela, Wilton Mkhwayi and I were allowed to go to a dentist in Cape Town. It was most unusual for the authorities to allow three prisoners off the Island. We then found a knife in the prison van at the docks. When we arrived our handcuffs were removed and the warder stayed outside the consulting room. We had planned to make a break then but called it off because we suspected a trap. When we looked into the surrounding streets, which were usually very busy, there were no cars or pedestrians in view, and we felt that the authorities might well use this attempted escape bid as an excuse to wipe us all out.

'Mac' Maharaj was born on 27th April 1935. He was arrested in 1964 and charged and convicted of sabotage. He spent 12 years on Robben Island. After the April 1994 election Maharaj was appointed Minister of Transport in the new Cabinet.

PRISONER 40/64

Jacob Zuma

I came to Robben Island in March 1964. When we arrived, the Chief Warder said to us in Afrikaans, 'This is Robben Island... everybody here has to tow the line... you might have come from other maximum security prisons like Red Hell, but this one is a Blue Hell'.

On our first day we were locked up in one of the cells in the old prison. We saw warders taking big sticks and clubs and getting ready for something we didn't understand. Then we saw a group of political prisoners being brought into the new cell block and being beaten up as they entered the gates. We shouted protests from our cell. Because of this they thought we needed a similar reception, so in the afternoon we were called into the yard where we were beaten for about 40 minutes. I remember an Indian comrade from Durban went up to a warder to say he couldn't take it any more. The warder promptly hit him hard and he fell to the ground. Then a prisoner in front of me, Andrew Masondo, was hit very hard on the back and as he fell he began bleeding. Andrew Masondo was often singled out for bad treatment, mainly because he was educated — he was a lecturer at Fort Hare — but also because he left his teaching to join MK. This was the treatment we got on the first day. We went to sleep that night not knowing what to expect the next day.

The prisoners all developed close bonds with one another. If one prisoner had a visitor, that person would have to repeat the entire experience to the other prisoners after the warders had locked up for the night. So those rare visits from outside were shared by many. That is one example of how close we were, as strong as a family unit. We were always very supportive of each other and would help anyone who was sick or who had family problems. We were there to console and comfort those who had lost family members and those few prisoners who couldn't take prison life.

Eventually it was my turn to leave the Island. I remember that it was a very painful and emotional process. We were leaving behind comrades who we had been with for ten years, and these people had become almost closer than our brothers. You had shared pain with them and had come to understand them very deeply. I remember that there was total silence on the boat leaving the Island because of this overwhelming emotion. But at the same time our resolve was strengthened to fight harder for the removal of this unjust system. Our motto and objective was that if you were a political prisoner on Robben Island you had better come off Robben Island a better politician, a better fighter.

Jacob Zuma was born on 12th April 1942. He was arrested in June 1963 and convicted of sabotage. He was sentenced to 15 years and spent the whole of his sentence on Robben Island, from 14th February 1964 to March 1979. After the April 1994 elections Zuma was appointed Social Welfare Minister in the Kwa Zulu/Natal Provincial Government.

PRISONER 14/86
Sfiso Buthelezi

I went to Robben Island in 1986 when I was 24 years old. I was a member of the military wing of the ANC and was involved in setting up MK bases to recruit and train people.

We knew that our heroes such as Mandela and Sisulu had been kept on the Island so we really equated Robben Island with freedom.

When I was arrested in 1984 I was put in solitary confinement under Section 29 of the Internal Security Act. The only people I could see were my interrogators, who were very hostile. It was a foregone conclusion that once you were arrested as a political prisoner you were going to be sent to the Island. When I got to Robben Island I found a community of people who thought the same way as I did and who were united in wanting to fight the Apartheid regime.

The prison authorities liked people to believe that they encouraged prisoners to study and when I came to the Island I registered for a Bachelor of Commerce degree, majoring in Economics. But my experience was that they didn't like to see us progressing academically. First you had to get a study privilege which involved making many applications. Then you had to sign a document which stipulated the conditions of study. One was that you were not allowed to study during the day, even if you'd finished your work. One example of the authorities not exactly encouraging our studies was when a comrade accidentally came across a pile of unreturned library books in a dustbin. We had borrowed these books from the UNISA library and the study office was meant to post them back. They punished the comrade who brought this matter to the attention of the authorities and withdrew his study privilege.

We used to look forward to visits, and we would start preparing a week before. You made sure your clothes were clean and ironed, your shoes polished. We also had a list of things which we wanted to ask our visitors. We knew that we only had 30 minutes, so we had to make the best of it — just imagine someone travelling all the way from Natal to find that you are only allocated 30 minutes. We pleaded with the warders to extend the visiting time but they didn't listen.

After I was released I went back to the Island to visit some of the comrades. When it was time to leave again it was a very sad moment.

Sfiso Buthelezi was born on 14th August 1961. He was sentenced to ten years for terrorism on 5th December 1985. He was released on 5th February 1991. Buthelezi then went on to study for a Master's degree in Economics at the University of Cape Town.

THE JAILER
Mike Green

One had to get used to the fact that basically you were also a prisoner on the Island... you could only get off the Island every other weekend. But the village is a very close-knit community. Once a warder's house burnt down. He didn't have any insurance, and within a week people had collected enough furniture to furnish a new house and some money. You don't get that in many places.

When I was transferred to the Island in 1980, I first worked with the prisoners and then moved to the Reception Office where my job was to purchase items for the prison shop. I was then head of Communications and I managed to increase the number of translators to cope with the prison visitors.

I'd been working with criminal prisoners for a long time and it was a total change for me to work with political prisoners. With criminal prisoners you couldn't leave money around, but it was quite a different story with political prisoners, who would probably return it to you. You wouldn't have to tell them to do things like clean their cells, as they had their own roster for cleaning the various sections. They basically did things their way rather than having to be told. It was a pleasure to work in the leadership section because those prisoners were very disciplined and when you requested that they go to the cells to be locked up you didn't have to request a second time. They'd move into their cells and close the doors for you, you just had to turn the key.

I discussed politics on various occasions with one of the prisoners, Tokyo Sexwale, and sometimes we agreed. I actually spoke to him after he left Robben Island when he was proclaimed the sexiest politician. We had a good laugh about that. It's funny to see how many of the prisoners I met on the Island might be, or will be, the leaders of the next government, because one didn't really think of that when one worked on the Island. One never thought of them eventually being your boss, but I haven't got a problem with that.

Mike Green was born on 10th June 1953. He came to Robben Island in December 1979 and worked in various departments. He was a warder in Mandela's section between 1980 and 1982. In 1994 Green was liaison officer for the Department of Correctional Services in the Western Cape.

61

PRISONER 72/79
Andrew Mapheto

Andrew Mapheto was charged with high treason and the trial lasted from 20th December 1978 to 14th November 1979. He was found guilty and spent 11 years and seven months on Robben Island.

I heard a guy on the Island playing a piece of music which I really liked and it was that song that made me learn to play the guitar. I learnt to play from a book and often composed my own songs to express my feelings.

I don't know if people can imagine what it's like to be in love and to be in prison — two very contradictory states — and one of my songs is an expression of that contradiction. Some of my music was lively, but some was quite sad.

I wrote one piece when I was on a hunger strike demanding the release of some prisoners. It was a very poignant moment for me — for the first time I was sitting with nothing to do as we couldn't do anything physical, and I decided to write a piece of music.

I played on my own and in a trio with another classical guitarist and a flautist and we usually played classical music. We practiced mainly in the bathroom and played to an audience at cultural events.

THE PRISON BAND
Roots

Ronnie Mabena — Vocalist/Drums
Norman Yengeni — Lead Guitar — Left
Michael Matakata — Congas
Curtis Mhlanzi — Bass Guitar — Right
Thabang Zulu — Vocalist

Ronnie Mabena was the co-founder of a Robben Island Band called Roots. During his five-year imprisonment on the Island, Ronnie was also the violinist in another musical group called the Kitchen Ensemble which started in the prison scullery, using improvised instruments.

Music was an escape from the harshness of prison life and was a means of expressing human emotion. Prisoners held long debates on the politics of music and the role of culture as a weapon of struggle. They turned theory into practice by developing these disciplined musical groups.

Return to the Island

by ELINOR SISULU

Albertina Sisulu, followed by Walter Sisulu, steps off the ferry on to Robben Island.

Walter Sisulu and Andrew Mlangeni show their wives, Albertina and June, around Robben Island.

Cape Town's new waterfront is graced by elegantly renovated buildings painted in pastel cake-icing colours — apricot, pink and pale greens and blues. It is an incongruous setting for the nondescript building at the heart of the waterfront. Dull and uninteresting in comparison to its surroundings, the building, which is the property of the South African prison, marks the beginning of the boat journey to the infamous Robben Island.

On a mildly sunny November morning in 1993, a convoy of cars comes to a halt in front of the prison services building. Two young men in immaculate suits step smartly out of the the first car and open the back doors for the elderly couple inside. Another couple emerges from the second car. The two couples, surrounded by bodyguards and a film crew, attract curious stares from passers-by. Few are aware of the significance of the occasion — ANC leaders and former Robben Island prisoners, Walter Sisulu and Andrew Mlangeni, on an historic visit to the Island with their wives, Albertina and June.

The group is ushered into a waiting room by polite but anxious prison officials. Albertina Sisulu and June Mlangeni recall the countless times they sat in the stark waiting room with red polished floors so typical of South African government buildings. Painful memories come flooding back...

While their husbands struggled to survive the harsh conditions of Robben Island, Albertina and June faced their own form of imprisonment in the vast prison that

◁ The crossing from Cape Town to Robben Island takes about 40 minutes. The sea is often rough and the boat rolls heavily, loaded with prisoners' families as well as warders and their wives, returning from shopping trips to Cape Town.

Docking at Robben Island harbour. The Prison Department runs the ferry and the harbour. The pier is cluttered with rusty, antique cars and trucks — cars do not need to be licensed on the Island.

was South Africa, and they were victimised by a hostile government in whose eyes they were guilty by association.

When their husbands were on trial, Albertina and June had to summon almost superhuman strength to face the possibility that the men might be sentenced to death. Walter remembers Albertina's response: 'Before the sentence was announced we were told by Joel (Joffe) that we might be sentenced to death. She told me, "My dear, you must be strong. Don't disgrace us".' June remembers defence lawyer George Bizos urging them not to shed tears in court if the death sentence was passed because, 'You must show these people how brave you are'.

The day after the Rivonia trialists were sentenced to life imprisonment, June travelled with Tiny Nokwe, the wife of Duma Nokwe, to Pretoria to try and see Andrew. 'As we approached the prison we saw a person on the upper floors wave to us. He dropped a piece of paper out of the window. It was a note which said the men had been taken to Robben Island at 3 o'clock that morning.'

'We were officially informed of this three months later when we received letters outlining the procedures to visit Robben Island. My letter contained a permit to visit Andrew and said I should go through the authorities. I did not know who these authorities were so I went to the Dube superintendent. He did not understand the letter either but he signed the permit'.

The Sisulus recreate a prison visit.

Common law prisoners chopping wood. Barbed wire fences surround the prison and a three-metre wide corridor is guarded during the night by large dogs such as Rottweilers.

The Sisulus and Mlangenis walk around the harbour.

Andrew Mlangeni and Walter Sisulu lead their wives through the lime quarry where they worked day after day for over ten years.

June had to find money to travel. 'This was difficult because I had been fired when someone told the bosses that my husband was involved in the Rivonia Trial. But somehow, I managed to scrape together enough money to get to Cape Town.' Albertina faced an extra set of obstacles: 'We were told we would only be allowed to visit if we had IDs. In those days it took months to get an ID. I believe they delayed my application deliberately. They would ask, "Where were you when other people were taking reference books?" As a result I only got to see Walter after five months.'

When Albertina was released from detention in 1963, she was banned for five years. Her banning orders compounded the already difficult process of visiting Robben Island. 'I first had to apply for a permit for Robben Island. I would then have to take this permit to the Chief Magistrate of Johannesburg, who in turn would inform the police. Before I left Johannesburg, I would have to report to the nearest police station to say I was on the way to the train station!' The police kept close watch during the journey. 'I used to be in third class and my police escort was in second class. They wanted to make sure I would not be part of any gathering of people during the course of the journey. Once in Cape Town I had to go to the police station at Caledon Square to tell them I had arrived, and show them my visiting permit. I also had to tell them where I would be staying.'

Walter Sisulu at the lime quarry where he taught political history to his fellow prisoners.

Albertina and Walter Sisulu sit in the ▷ contact visiting room. Sisulu was only allowed contact visits in the latter part of this prison term.

Now the two couples are returning to Robben Island, not as prisoners or prisoners' wives, but as dignitaries. Everything is different. Even the ferry boat is different. Albertina and June comment on how comfortable and new the *Penguin* is — a contrast to the *Susan Kruger* which was an old river boat reconstructed to make it seaworthy. It was very slow and uncomfortable.

Albertina has very unpleasant memories of her first boat trip. 'Before you got to the boat, you had to go through the office to show your permit. What a long process! The queue! Most of the people were visiting common law prisoners. Conditions were terrible. It was my first time on a boat. The sea was rough. I could not stand the smell. I vomited all the way. I was so miserable.'

June was even less fortunate on her first visit. 'The train from Johannesburg was delayed. We got to Cape Town at 2 o'clock and the boat to the Island had left at midday. I finally took a taxi to the docks and was told I could not go to the Island. I explained my situation and asked if I could go the next day, but they refused. I

The exercise yard for the isolation cells. In the early days political prisoners had to break up stones in the yard. Much later it was used for playing ball games.

Prison guards standing in front of the ▷ section which housed the main body of political prisoners who were kept in overcrowded cells.

had to go back home and start the long process of applying for a visit from scratch'.

On this trip there are about 50 people on the boat. They look like commuters going to work. There are a number of tall, well-built young men who could be warders. One of them approaches, his hand held out in a friendly greeting. He introduces himself as the chaplain of Robben Island and gives Sisulu a card.

The journey to Robben Island takes 40 minutes. We are told it can take up to two hours if the weather is bad. We are fortunate, it is a fine day and we sit back to enjoy the scenery. To the left we see the Gardens and the City Bowl. To the right is Bloubergstrand. We drink in the extraordinary beauty of the mountains which dominate Cape Town's landscape. Albertina and June say they never appreciated the view when their husbands were prisoners. They were too preoccupied with anticipating the precious 30 minutes, and in any case they had to sit on the lower decks where they could not see anything.

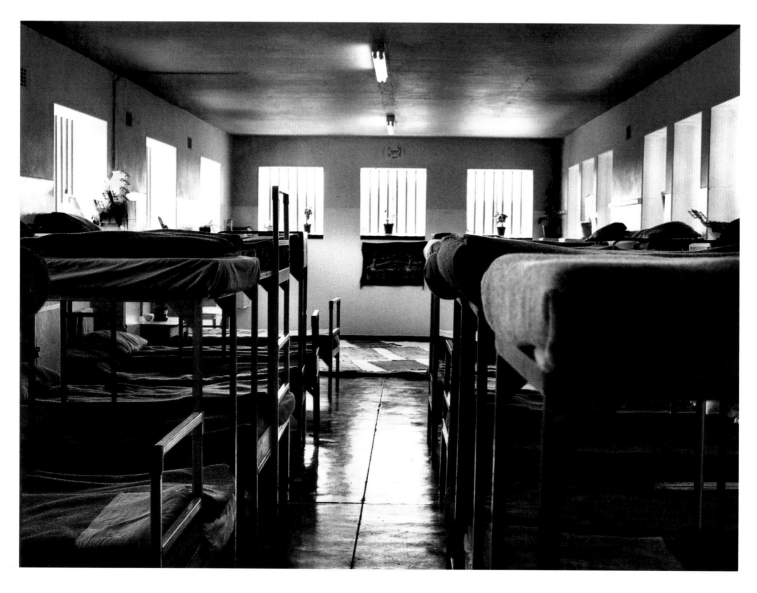

The boat arrives at the Island and pulls into Murray's Harbour. As we disembark Andrew recognises one of the warders. The two men greet each other enthusiastically.

A young warder is assigned to act as our tour guide. He leads us to the visitors block, a bungalow style building in the harbour area. As one enters the building there is a waiting room to the right. On the left a line of small rectangular cubicles open off the passage. These are for visitors. Through a thick pane of glass is a mirror image cubicle for the prisoners. There is a telephone on either side of the glass. Behind the prisoners' cubicles are the prisoners' waiting rooms, tiny square rooms with heavy steel doors.

The tiny rooms look cramped and unfriendly but we are assured that they are a vast improvement on the days when visits took place in the open. As the two couples reconstruct a typical visit for the film crew, Walter and Andrew become prisoners again. Falling easily into old roles, Albertina and June update their husbands on the progress of children in schools, the payment of school fees, and the general well-being of their families. It is just like old times — which they are glad to have left behind.

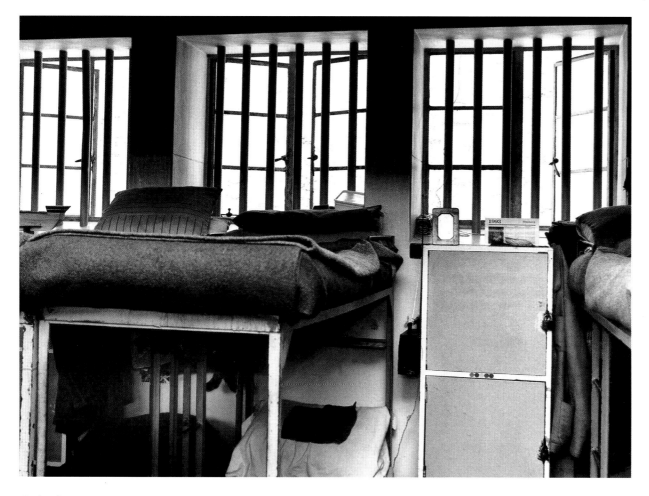

During the 1970s and 1980s this cell held as many as 70 prisoners. It now holds 36 narrow bunks.

'I will never forget my first visit', says Albertina. 'We were led to the open veld. There was a fence and a table next to which a policeman stood. Our men were on one side of the fence and we were on the other. We were a group of about 20. Everyone talked at the same time. We had to shout to make ourselves heard. The noise would reach a peak and the policeman would bang on the table. There would be silence and then it would start all over again.'

Conversations were carefully monitored. If they discussed anything other than family matters the visit was terminated immediately. 'In those first years we never had a complete visit because they interrupted time and time again.'

Albertina and June visited Robben Island regularly until their husbands were transferred to Pollsmoor Prison on the Cape mainland in 1982. As the conditions of political prisoners improved, the rules and regulations surrounding visits became more lenient. Visits became more frequent and of longer duration, until eventually prisoners were allowed the luxury of contact visits. In 1982 Albertina and June had their first contact visits — they sat in the same room and touched their husbands for the first time in 18 years.

The Sisulus and Mlangenis wander through the warders' village where 250 staff members live with their families.

From the visiting block we are taken by bus to the famous quarry. En route we pass the common law prison which still houses several hundred prisoners. There is a brief stop at the administrative offices where the film crew tries to negotiate permission to enter the cells of Walter Sisulu and Andrew Mlangeni. The response is an unequivocal no and we proceed to the quarry.

At the entrance to the quarry are piles of garbage — old shoes, tin cans, bits of scrap metal and building debris. Andrew Mlangeni is dismayed. 'Good lord! They have turned this place into a dumping ground', he exclaims. 'When we worked here it was spotless!' Walking across the quarry, Walter and Andrew reminisce about the many years they spent there. 'The lime quarry, my dear', says Andrew to June, with a theatrical wave of the arm. 'People such as Makana used to work here. We did everything here, education, politics, everything.' Standing in the middle of the basin-shaped quarry, the familiar stories of their days of hard labour are more vivid and real.

We then move on to the warder's canteen and lunch, and then a tour of the village. Albertina and June are surprised at the size of the Island. 'I didn't know it was so big,' says Albertina. 'To us it was just a small area. It is also surprising to see a village with people living there.' The place is also unfamiliar to Walter and

The old church in the centre of a deserted village. The Island, exposed to the South West and Antarctic gales, is windy, cold, wet and grey.

Andrew because, unlike common law prisoners who often did domestic and gardening work in the warders' houses, political prisoners seldom saw the village.

The village boasts comfortable sturdy houses and a beautiful old school building. It is difficult to imagine that the bleak prison buildings a short distance away are the *raison d'etre* for this tranquil village. At the village shop Albertina and June buy souvenirs of the Island — tiny spoons bearing the Robben Island emblem.

All too soon we have to rush back to the boat. We arrive at the harbour in the nick of time. On the return journey June and Albertina agree that this is one visit to the Island which will bring back happy memories. 'I felt like a queen,' says June, 'I never imagined I would have lunch in the warders' mess or see the quarry where my husband worked for so many years.' Albertina comments on the attitude of the prison staff: 'They were very nice. You would not think those were the people who treated us like prisoners.'

As if to add emphasis to her words, the chaplain who had greeted them on the outward journey comes up to them again. He talks of the need for love and reconciliation between all people. They nod in agreement.

The children's playground in the warders' village is sandy, desolate and bare.

77

The village school for children of warders and administrators. Every morning they raise the South African flag and sing Die Stem.

WARDERS ON THE ISLAND

'There's nobody to bother you, you're on you own. It's just lekker.'

'Robben Island is like a big family.'

'I usually tell the people in Cape Town that I'm from overseas.'

'You don't have to lock your doors or windows when you go to sleep.'

The warders' pub, filled with boeremusiek and animated conversation. The TV set in the corner was ignored until Nelson Mandela appeared on the news and then all eyes were fixed on the screen. Loud cries of 'Viva, Viva' emanated from the dart players in the corner.

The Commander of Robben Island, Colonel Mike de Nysschen, taking the salute at a presentation of medals to warders who have served for over ten years.

The population of Robben Island is about 1 300 people — this includes 244 personnel, 300 other members of their families and a prison population of about 750.

The restaurant run by the prison department is frequented by the warders and their families.

Nelson Mandela
Returns to Robben Island

by ENOCH SITHOLE

Mandela's cell (left and above), where he spent most of his 18 years on the Island.

'Welcome to Robben Island, We serve with Pride' — states the notice on the gate of the prison where Nelson Mandela, his comrade Walter Sisulu, and several others spent almost two decades.

As Mandela and other ex-Rivonia trialists returned on 11th February 1994 to celebrate the fourth anniversary of his release and to shoot footage for an American TV documentary, they were indeed served with pride — by the very men who had held them captive. This time, they did not arrive chained together, as they had been on that cold and windy morning of 14th June 1964, aboard a military jet that flew them from Waterkloof Air Force base in Pretoria.

Despite the chains they had felt some relief — they had left Pretoria Central prison and its warders who seemed to take great delight in tormenting their political prisoners. Robben Island was a prison, but it was as well the only home they would have until their deaths. Their relief was short-lived, as they were soon to discover.

One night, shortly after their arrival, drunken prison warders burst into the cell which housed Mandela, Sisulu, Govan Mbeki, Ahmed Kathrada, Andrew Mlangeni, Wilton Mkhwayi, Raymond Mhlaba and Elias Motsoaledi. The prisoners were woken roughly and ordered to stand naked against the wall. These and other incidents were now the subject of memory. 'This time I know that I am going back home, and I know when', said Nelson Mandela, 'I can leave... whenever I want to'.

Mandela, on foot, led the TV crew to various spots on the island — along the edge of the sea, to the quarry where he had worked, into the prison courtyard, and then on to the mosque. At noon the group was joined by a bevy of journalists who had crossed to the Island by boat. Lunch was a prestigious affair. The venue was the one used for visiting dignitaries — cabinet ministers, directors-general and other visiting VIPs. On this day a line of tall, clean-shaven warders stood to attention as Mandela took his seat. They too, indicated a sensitivity, in a more informal moment, to the way that times had changed. 'We are honoured to have him here', one said.

Lunch for Mandela, this time round, was one of choices — orange juice or soda water instead of 'the brown stuff', and chicken, peas and baked potato instead of boiled mealies. Not that he could enjoy it at leisure — journalists jostled and pushed, all trying for a shot of Mandela eating.

Nelson Mandela on a visit to Robben Island on the fourth anniversary of his release from prison in February 1990. Over lunch Mandela tells the story of the pain he experienced in prison on hearing of his mother's death. He was not allowed to attend her funeral.

Although pushed to do so, Mandela was reluctant to talk about his personal experiences and feelings. 'All that happened to me and what I have achieved is a team effort', he said. But he did provide a few insights. With bowed head he explained that 'the biggest psychological persecution I experienced was the death of my mother, Mosekeni Fanny, in 1968. When she came to visit me a few months before she died, she did not look too well, and it came to my thoughts that I was seeing her for the last time'. When his father, and then his son, had died, Mandela had remained silent. Now he asked his jailers the impossible — to be allowed to travel to Transkei to bury his mother. Predictably, the authorities refused, arguing that should his supporters see him off Robben Island there would be turmoil. This refusal caused him great pain, but 'I knew that if they caught me for my involvement, they would punish me in whatever way they wanted', he said.

In passing, and this time with a smile, Mandela mentioned other privations. For over four of the years he spent on Robben Island he slept on a one centimetre thick mattress placed on the cold cement of the cell floor. For approximately 15 years he lived without underwear, wore shoes without socks, and was not allowed to wear long pants.

After lunch Mandela led journalists to the quarry where the long-term prisoners had spent their days crushing stones. In some ways, he said, 'We succeeded in turning our suffering into happiness — we sang revolutionary songs as we worked and we debated matters of national importance. Singing made us overcome the pain of the work we were doing'. Mandela, Mlangeni, Sisulu and Kathrada then

Govan Mbeki, Nelson Mandela and Andrew Mlangeni surrounded by journalists in the square inside the prison where they were held for many years.

sang a short chorus from *Shosholoza* in demonstration. But even talking was not really allowed during those long, tiring days of hard labour. 'I remember that one day while we were working with comrade Andrew Masondo, we got involved in a debate on whether there were tigers in South Africa. A young warden came and accused me of talking too much instead of working. There was nothing I could do, I was sentenced to a spare diet for several days'.

A moment of obvious emotion — Mandela entered the cell where he had slept for 18 years. Furnished only with a narrow bed, the 2 x 2,5 metre cell had cream walls and a small barred window at shoulder height looking out over the courtyard. The door was of thick wood and next to it looking out into the passage was a small barred window. Mandela spent over an hour there, taking questions, being photographed, and throughout looking a little sad, clearly remembering the many, many hours spent within the confines of those narrow walls. This was all the space he had to study for his LLB degree, do push-ups in the morning to keep fit, and to reflect on his reason for being in prison — his goal to liberate his people from the injustices of Apartheid. There were some small advantages: 'Well, prison gave me the opportunity to think through many issues. I also had the time to debate issues with my comrades. That is no longer possible in the life I lead now'.

It was time to return to the mainland, and wreathed in smiles, Mandela led the way to the ferry which was to carry us back to Cape Town. Someone asked what he had to say as a conclusion to this visit. 'Never again', he said, 'never again will anybody be kept here for the reasons that we were kept here'.

The Man and his Boat:

Attempted Escapes from Robben Island

by CHARLENE SMITH

The Cape Peninsula stretches around Robben Island like a cupped hand. Bloubergstrand extends a beckoning finger, a deceitful finger, because once trapped within the seemingly placid lake that shimmers between Robben Island and the mainland, one realises the treachery of the bitterly cold, churning ocean.

Many incarcerated on Robben Island over the centuries have responded to the invitation of the finger and perished, but many others have escaped in boxes, rafts, animal hide boats, hi-jacked schooners and paddle-skis.

Toward the end of Queen Victoria's reign an old man, possibly destitute or ill, was among the Cape's human flotsam who were dumped on the Island. The cruelty of the mainland evaded him, it was life instead that beckoned. Plaatjes scoured the beaches for planks and steel from shipwrecks. He would sit apart from the other inhabitants of the Island, near a favoured clump of bushes, and quietly begin hammering out the skeleton of a boat. Hospital staff would keep an eye on him, and as Plaatjes began lovingly adding the final touches to his boat, they would take it from him and burn it.

Plaatjes would watch sadly. Once the last ash wisps of his boat had taken flight in the wind across the bay, he would rise and head again for the beaches, gathering brass to hammer out flat coins which he would carve with a likeness of Queen Victoria. Once he had exhausted all his brass, he would search for more planks for another boat. This Plaatjes did, in an unending cycle, until at last death rescued him from the Island.

Few remember Plaatjes. There is a tantalising photograph of him in the archives, but historical records are all but devoid of information on him.

The most famous escape attempt occured in 1819. The great Xhosa prophet Nxele Makana led an abortive raid on Grahamstown in that year and he was jailed on Robben Island. He immediately became part of a group hatching escape plans.

It seems preparations were well underway by the time he arrived. Two prisoners, John Smith and a man called Holmes had devised a simple plan. One morning a guard opened their cells and was rushed at by about 30 prisoners, who stole his weapons. A brief skirmish ensued as other warders rushed to his aid, but the prisoners had the advantage of numbers. They ran to John Murray's nearby whaling station, leapt into a longboat and rowed furiously for Bloubergstrand beach.

However, the boat collided with the rocks that fence Bloubergstrand beach and most were drowned. Legend has it that Makana clung to a rock shouting encouragement to his comrades before he drowned. Smith and two other ringleaders were caught. They were hanged, then decapitated and their heads fixed to stakes on the Island, as a warning to others.

A successful escape requires patience, guile, hours of observation and courage. Few had all of these skills as perfectly honed as Autshumao. A Khoikhoi beachcomber, he had spent time as a sailor on a passing Dutch ship and was fluent in Dutch. After Van Riebeeck established his settlement at the Cape in 1652, Autshumao offered his services and quickly became invaluable. But Autshumao, also had a political agenda — he was soon deftly playing the Dutch off against the Khoikhoi and spreading his own power base. Finally, the Dutch

Plaatjes, a mental patient, sitting in the boat he built in the hope of escaping from Robben Island.

Photograph: Cape Archives

banished him to Robben Island. But they either never knew, or had forgotten, that the Khoikhoi had commuted between Robben Island and the Cape for generations. Escape was easy for Autshumao. He and another prisoner fashioned a boat from skins and let the tide carry them northward to a beach near Saldanha Bay. Months later he arrived on Van Riebeeck's doorstep bearing gifts, asking for his job back. He was pardoned and resumed his duties. Over the years he was exiled to Robben Island on a few occasions, but always managed to escape and was always ultimately pardoned.

Eddie Daniels, who was imprisoned in B Section with Nelson Mandela and the Rivonia trialists, was fond of dreaming of ways to escape. His most ambitious plan was toward the end of his incarceration in 1979. If it had worked, or failed, it would have dramatically altered the course of South African history.

Daniels' plan was that a helicopter, not unusual in a bay where aircraft are used daily to retrieve or take items to vessels, should hover over the prison courtyard and lower a basket for Mandela and Walter Sisulu to climb into. It would then take them to an embassy on the mainland, one that was well-disposed toward the ANC, for the men to claim asylum. They would then be smuggled from that embassy into exile. Daniels presented his plan to Mandela, who discussed it with his jailed compatriots from Umkhonto we Sizwe High Command. They assented to the plans, if ANC High Command in exile gave it the green light. It was decided though, that Sisulu would remain on the Island to continue leading and directing ANC affairs within the country from inside prison. Daniels then recommended that Swapo founder and leader, Andimba Herman Toivo ja Toivo be liberated with Mandela.

The escape was planned for 9.15 am on New Year's Day 1981. Not only would warders, Daniels reasoned, probably be suffering from hangovers, but they would be busy with visitors who would arrive from 9 am. Daniels believed that by the time warders realised what was going on, it would be too late for them to take action. If aircraft had time to scramble, the escapers would already be over built up areas, which, he reasoned, would lessen the likelihood of the airforce opening fire. Daniels had little faith in the warders' ability to shoot and kill the escapers, or to damage the helicopter.

On his release from prison in November 1979, Daniels was instructed to explain the plot to the ANC in exile. However, a banning order made it impossible for him to travel or leave the country. Instead he wrote his plan on fine paper, then carefully slit and sealed a postcard with the plan inside. He gave it to a friend, Moira Henderson, who was visiting London. She was told to give the card to Randolph Vigne, who had been in the African Resistance Movement with Daniels. The card instructed Vigne to pass it on to Oliver Tambo with instructions to treat the postcard in the same way as a photo album Daniels had sent before. It too had pages slit and thin notes concealed within them.

He heard nothing further from Tambo or London, so assumed his cryptic message had not been understood or the plan ignored. In fact, it had been studied but, perhaps fortunately for history and the lives of Mandela and Toivo ja Toivo, it was never seriously considered as an option by the ANC.

Robben Island

a dramatised documentary based on historical records
and testimonies of prisoners

by MARY BENSON

Broadcast by the SABC's Monday Night Playhouse in
November 1992 and March 1993

Production directed by ALAN SWERDLOW

(SEA, FADED AND HELD UNDER)

NARRATOR: Robben Island, in the Atlantic Ocean off Cape Town, has become as notorious as Devil's Island. Two-and-a-half miles long by one-and-a-half miles wide, the Island lies some seven miles to the north-west of Cape Town but appears much nearer. Passengers on ships bound for the Cape know they have arrived when they see the lighthouse on the Island or, in fog, hear its siren. At night, the beam of that lighthouse is part of Cape Town's seafront panorama.

(BRING UP SEAS)

The seas around the Island can be rough. *'Tormentoso'* the Portuguese navigator Bartolomeu Dias named the Cape in 1488, because of the perils and storms. But his King Joâo gave it a more illustrious name because it promised the discovery of India, land of spices: *Cabo de Boa Esperançe*, Cape of Good Hope. In 1503 Antonio de Saldanha landed there, and sent a boatload of men to explore the small island in the bay.

PORTUGUESE NAVIGATOR: We killed many birds which are called *sotilicário*, or penguins and seawolves and tortoises, of which there was great abundance. Later in the sixteenth century came Dutch navigators, then English and French, on their journeys to the Indies in search of fabled spices.
After five months at sea and many deaths from the scurvy, they were desperate for fresh meat.

DUTCH NAVIGATOR: I went to see the Island: very sandy, no water. The bushes are full of yellow blossoms. We drove about 600 penguins to our vessels. They allowed themselves to be driven like sheep.

FRENCH NAVIGATOR: Penguins do not at all taste like meat – I take them to be feathered fish.

ENGLISH NAVIGATOR: Penguins are a bird! The wings or fins hanging down like sleeves. A degenerate duck.

FRENCH NAVIGATOR: There are also many rats and grass-snakes, chameleons and other lizards. On the rocks, basking in the sun, great numbers of seabears are found, which bleat like sheep.

DUTCH NAVIGATOR: Our men amused themselves by clubbing fully 100 to death.

NARRATOR: These Dutch navigators called it Robben Island – seal island. Seals, penguins and rabbits were caught by the Dutch – but the Island remained uninhabited by humans. On the mainland were people who called themselves Khoikhoi – Men of Men. The Dutch called them Hüttentütt – stammerer – or Hottentot.

DUTCH NAVIGATOR: Their speech is just as if one heard a number of angry turkeys. They are short in stature, ugly of face, the hair on their heads often looking as if singed off by the sun. They go quite naked but for the tail of a small wild animal before their privates which are little covered by it.

ENGLISH NAVIGATOR: The people are not circumcised. They are all of a tawny colour, and are much given to pick and steal. They cluck with their tongues like a brood hen; the sharpest wit among us could not learn one word of their language; and yet the people would soon understand any signs we made to them.

NARRATOR: The English wanted to trade with the Khoikhoi: brass, iron, tobacco, brandy and beads, in exchange for cattle, for fat-tailed sheep, and dagga – marijuana. Sir Thomas Smythe, founder and governor of the English East India Company, and a leading financier in the City of London, had an idea: why not install Settlers at the Cape? He was inspired by Senior Merchant Thomas Aldworth, who said: 'I have never seen a better land. It is full of woods and lovely rivers, with much deer, fish and birds, and the abundance of cows and ewes is astounding. And we found the natives to be very courteous and tractable folk. Therefore, prudent persons of London should choose a hundred convicts each year, and send them to this new settlement – without doubt they would not lack friends'.

King James approved. It was the first time that transportation was attempted. The year: 1615. John Crosse was selected to lead these élite settlers from Newgate.

ENGLISH CAPTAIN:	John Crosse: found guilty of highway robbery on the London to St Alban's road. Item: a bay horse worth four pounds. Item: a cloak worth ten shillings. Item: a Bible worth two shillings. Item: sundry garments, twelve pence in money. Sentenced to be hanged. Crosse was given the choice: Tyburn gallows or the Cape of Good Hope. Our ship sailed with Crosse and nine other lewd malefactors. At the Cape we left them. We gave each man weapons for his own defence against wild beasts and men; also victuals. Crosse asked for and was given a boat. We then sailed on to the Indies.
NARRATOR:	The Khoikhoi watched the sailing of the ship, and noticed that these ten men were left behind. They were full of suspicion.
ENGLISH CAPTAIN:	Crosse, a very stout and resolute man, quarrelled with and abused the natives, whereupon these savages fell upon him, and with their darts and arrows shot at him.
NARRATOR:	One of his companions was killed. Crosse and the others escaped in their small boat and rowed to Robben Island. The seas were running high, their boat split on landing. They were stranded on the Island.
ENGLISH CAPTAIN:	A place wherein grows never a tree, either for sustenance or shelter, a place that hath never a drop of fresh water but what the showers leave in holes in the rocks. And besides, there are a great number of snakes – so many of those venomous worms that a man cannot tread safely. A place beyond measure uncomfortable to those most wretched men.
NARRATOR:	Some months later a passing ship attempted to rescue them, but Crosse and five others were drowned. In 1617 the British again transported convicts to the Cape and this time attempted to deposit them directly on Robben Island – but when they saw it, the men begged rather to be hanged than left in that God-forsaken place.

(SEA)

NARRATOR:	Soon the British gave up their attempt to settle at the Cape. Now, their rivals, the Dutch, got a stranglehold on the spice trade. In 1652 Jan van Riebeeck, with 90 men, landed at the Cape and built a small fort on the mainland. It was to be a halfway station for ships of the Dutch East India Company. The Company was Mammon to these men and they were its faithful servants. Commander Van Riebeeck gave his instructions.
VAN RIEBEECK:	In negotiating for the goods of the inhabitants, you must not be too free and liberal, as frequently our worse merchandise is by them esteemed the most valuable. However, to allure them, you may at first be somewhat more liberal. That is, provided you cannot succeed otherwise.
NARRATOR:	Van Riebeeck and the Dutch relied on an interpreter, one of the Khoikhoi, whom they called Herry. For years, Herry haunted the journals kept by Van Riebeeck.
DUTCHMAN 1:	Today Herry again delivered two beautiful fat beasts and three sheep.
DUTCHMAN 2:	We have been mightily deceived by Herry. We fed him from our table, and clothed him in Dutch attire.
DUTCHMAN 1:	Whatever Herry may be conspiring with the people in the interior is difficult to tell. One can surmise he is doing little good. About 50 natives declared boldly that this was not our land but theirs! It is becoming more and more evident that these rogues are emboldened by kind treatment.
DUTCHMAN 2:	Not a single Hottentot is kindly disposed towards Herry, he is such a big talker and is continually carrying false reports from one side to the other.
DUTCHMAN 1:	However, if he keeps faith he may be acknowledged as Chief of the Hottentots.

DUTCHMAN 2:	Herry appeared shivering like a lady's lapdog. The commander gave him a cup of sherry, his companions were treated with arrack. Upon this they and their wives commenced to jump and dance, and left us in good spirits. We trust that in bringing in cattle, Herry will show that there is some good in him.
DUTCHMAN 1:	Herry who, by dint of his thefts and faithlessness had become a petty King, we have expelled from his Kingdom, deprived of all his cattle, and placed him as an exile on Robben Island ....
NARRATOR:	Herry had been found guilty of striking the first blow against a Dutch herdboy who was then murdered by other Khoikhoi. He was placed in the charge of the Superintendent who had recently been appointed to oversee the Island. It was July 1658.
VAN RIEBEECK:	Johan van Riebeeck, from the Fort de Goede Hoop, to Ryck Overhagen, Superintendent of Robben Island: 'You will herewith receive the late interpreter Herry, with the Hottentots Jan Cou and Boubo, whom you will keep on the Island, and employ upon such work as may suit their inclinations, without using force to compel them to any thing'.
NARRATOR:	The following year Herry escaped from the Island in a leaky fishing boat. Amazingly, he survived. He took part in Khoikhoi wars against the Dutch. Yet, at the end of his life, he was again interpreter for them.
	Meanwhile, Van Riebeeck had granted lands to the first free Burghers, nine men, Dutch and German, in 1657. Slaves were imported from Madagascar and Malaya to work for them. From the start, the Dutch found wives and mistresses among the Khoikhoi and among the slaves. Three of the first Superintendents of Robben Island had black wives. One was Surgeon Pieter van Meerhoff, who married Herry's niece, Eva, an interpreter for the Dutch at the age of 17, and the first Christian convert among the Khoikhoi. When, in 1667, her husband was killed in Madagascar, Eva and her children left Robben Island for the mainland.
NARRATOR:	In 1638 a captain had planted 109 coconuts on Robben Island, and lemon pips and pumpkin seeds. None germinated. Under Commander Van Riebeeck fresh efforts were made; also, a herd of sheep was placed there. Corporal Marcus Robbeljaert – in charge of them – addressed his commander:
ROBBELJAERT:	Know hereby, My Lord, that all goes well on the Island and six lambs have been born. The cabbage plants are growing well, likewise the carrots. The wheat also is green on the land. We are also sending Your Honour 59 goose eggs. Would Your Honour please send us one or two rattles for we cannot keep the ravens and geese out. Lastly, we, Your Honour's servants, wish Your Honour a thousand times goodnight.
NARRATOR:	The wind withered the wheat. Pigs brought to the Island died. The sheep multiplied to 600, then 500 of them died. Only the rabbits flourished, so much so that a greyhound was brought there to keep them down.

(SEA)

It was Van Riebeeck's successor, Zacharias Wagenaar, who recognised the potential of the Island as a prison:

DUTCHMAN:	The prisoners are not in public view. They serve their term of hard labour with chains clamped around their wrists and ankles. The sea not only keeps them from escaping, it keeps unwanted visitors out.
NARRATOR:	The prisoners were men and women, Hottentot, Dutch, Malay ....
DUTCHMAN:	Stealing sheep, food, fruit or picking pockets, housebreaking or stabbing, mutiny, murder – landed them on the Island in chains for anything up to 50 years.
NARRATOR:	Or for life. In 1672 two slaves who had stolen vegetables had their ears cut off and were kept in chains until they died. The prisoners broke stone in the quarries and collected shells for lime. Blue stone from the Island was used for the *stoeps* and stairways of the graceful Dutch homes on the mainland.

DUTCHWOMAN:	Thuintjie van Warden, wife of a Burgher, found guilty of evil speaking against other women, was sentenced to retract the slander, to ask for forgiveness, to be bound to a post for one hour, and – for six weeks – to suffer banishment to Robben Island.
DUTCHMAN:	I received a report from the Island that the five Hottentots confined there for sheep stealing and assault have escaped in a small boat; truly a very bold undertaking for such savages to trust themselves to such a distance in so small a *jolletjie*, with only two oars and no rudder. It is a proof of the strong desire for freedom which exists in a state of slavery.
NARRATOR:	South Africa's first white settler, one of those nine Burghers who were granted land behind Table Mountain, was Willem Willems:
WILLEMS:	'Petition to His Highness the Prince of Orange: I, Willem Willems, freeman and farmer of *Caap de Bona Esperançe*, the first who began to cultivate land there, most humbly show, that on the 28 April of the present year 1672, a Hottentot, a savage, entered my house and therein wilfully broke in pieces a beer mug; I, becoming very much provoked, took my gun, which was loaded with nothing but powder, and fired after the Hottentot, to give him a fright, but there having been some small shot among the powder, the said Hottentot was wounded, and died in four days. I seek grace and pardon for the said unintentional act'.
CORNELISSEN:	I, Ockert Cornelissen, declare that on a certain day in April in the year 1672, at which time I resided with W. Willems, when I was cooking the victuals, a certain Hottentot, being about to do something or other, laid down his covering, the skin of a sheep or other animal, upon an oven, and when taking it up again, from carelessness, pulled down and broke an earthenware mug which contained water. The said Willem Willems, on learning that the jug had been broken, set his dogs upon the person of the said Hottentot and, having fetched out a fowling piece, followed the now fugitive Hottentot round the house..(TO WILLEMS) Willem, what are you about, whose gun are you shooting with?
WILLEMS:	(TO CORNELISSEN) With my gun, there is only loose powder in it.
CORNELISSEN:	I assure you I thought it mine which hangs upon the wall loaded with a large-sized small shot. Soon after, I heard a shot fired, and saw the Hottentot fall down. (TO WILLEMS) Master! What are you about, you have shot the Hottentot?
WILLEMS:	I am certain I hit him, for I aimed at his middle.
CORNELISSEN:	You have made a pretty business of it.
WILLEMS:	Well, what does it signify?
GOVERNOR:	High-born and illustrious Prince. We the Governor and Council state that all the main positions taken up in the delinquent Willem Willems' petition, have been found to be frivolous, fabricated and utterly irreconcilable with the truth. Therefore we resolved to detain the delinquent on Robben Island.
NARRATOR:	Three years later, in 1676 —
GOVERNOR:	The afternoon Council considered: the free man, Willem Willems, having been kept upon Robben Island, when it became necessary to bring him to the mainland to be cured of the dropsy; and his wife – who, during his absence lived a very loose and unchaste life, having borne two children in adultery to a certain free Burgher named Ockert Cornelissen – is now in no way disposed to live in peace with her husband. Resolved therefore to send the said Willem Willems and his wife to Batavia, but apart from each other, and that the said Ockert Cornelissen shall be placed on Robben Island.

(SEA)

NARRATOR:	In the eighteenth century a variety of notable men connected with the Indies and the Pacific found themselves on the Island, for various reasons: Lord Clive, en route to India, was driven ashore by the South-Easter, and had to spend a night there. And Captain Cook went there in search of rabbits, for New Zealand. One of his company, Forster, observed, 'This Island is a barren and sandy spot where many murderers and miscreants are confined by the Dutch East Indies Company. Among them, however, are some unhappy victims of the merciless ambitions of these merchants: Rajahs, Sheiks and Princes of Java and the Moluccas who were exiled by the Dutch to this Island'.

(SEA)

	In 1806 the British, at war with the Dutch, occupied the Cape. They found themselves responsible for the governance of 16 000 Europeans and 17 000 slaves, as well as an indeterminate number of the Khoikhoi – often, now, vagrants or under-paid farm labourers. And they found themselves saddled with the Frontier problem; in the Eastern Cape there were sporadic skirmishes with the Xhosa people over boundaries and cattle. Governor Sir Charles Somerset decided to import settlers from Britain as the cheapest way of securing that frontier. An unusual settler spoke up for the Xhosa people: Thomas Pringle, Scottish poet, who was to become the champion of a free press and an abolitionist.
PRINGLE:	The Caffer tribes are a tall, athletic and handsome race of men. Their colour is a clear dark brown. Their address is frank, cheerful and manly. Their government is patriarchal. The clothing of both sexes consists entirely of the skins of animals, their arms are the assegai or javelin, a short club and a large shield of hide. The wars between the contiguous tribes are seldom very bloody. The females are seldom slain, and in their conflict with the colonists, there are many well-known examples of their humanity towards females who had fallen into their hands.
NARRATOR:	A prophet and leader arose among the Xhosa people: his name, Makana, the year, 1819.
COLONIST'S WIFE:	Makana is a witchdoctor who is to the kaffir nation what Mahomet was to the Arabs. Kaffirs are carried away with his most extraordinary fanaticism.
PRINGLE:	Makana delights to converse with Mr Vanderlingen, the chaplain, to elicit information in regard to the doctrines of Christianity and to puzzle him in return with metaphysical subtleties or mystical ravings. He is also in the habit of visiting the British headquarters at Graham's Town, and envinces an insatiable curiosity and an acute intellect. With the military officers he talks of war, or of such of the mechanical arts as fall under his notice.
NARRATOR:	When the Colonial troops, in support of a renegade Chief, ravaged Xhosa lands and herds, Makana spoke for his people:
MAKANA:	The war, British Chiefs, is an unjust one, for you are striving to extirpate a people whom you forced to take up arms. Our fathers were men; they loved their cattle; their wives and children lived on milk; they fought for their property. They began to hate the Colonists, who coveted their all, and aimed at their destruction. You came at last like locusts. We stood; we could do no more.
	We wish for peace; we wish to rest in our huts; we wish to get milk for our children; our wives wish to till the land. But your troops cover the plains and swarm in the thickets, where they cannot distinguish the man from the woman, and shoot all.
NARRATOR:	Makana led an attack on Graham's Town. In broad daylight thousands of Xhosa warriors swept down on the small British garrison.
COLONIST'S WIFE:	Imagine we are among that surging swaying horde of savage warriors. We see the gleam of the fire in their eyes. We shudder at the fearful, and once heard never-to-be-forgotten, war-cry as it is taken up by the whole host as they brandish their assegais. Makana inflames them with the madness that consumes himself: 'To battle! To battle! Let us drive the accursed white man beyond the Zwartkop's River and into the ocean, and then we shall stay our hand, and sit down and eat honey'.

NARRATOR:	In the bitter fighting Xhosa assegais fell short or were ineffectual against the British guns.
COLONIST'S WIFE:	The story of how the stream ran red with the blood of Makana's braves has been told in every nursery in Graham's Town!
PRINGLE:	Throughout the colony the burgher militia were called out to assist in chastising the 'savages'. Threatened with extermination if they did not deliver up Makana and their chiefs 'dead or alive', the Caffer people yet remained faithful. Driven to despair, perishing for want, yet not one was willing to earn the high reward offered. The course adopted by Makana in these circumstances was remarkable.
NARRATOR:	The British Commander described what happened:
STOCKENSTROM:	I was encamped with my division on the high ground east of Trompetter's Drift on the Great Fish River when to my surprise Chief Makana walked unattended into the camp, with an air of calm pride and self-possession which commanded involuntary respect.
MAKANA:	People say that I have occasioned the war? Let me see whether my delivering myself up to the conquerors will restore peace to my country.
PRINGLE:	Makana was bound, and the British condemned him to be imprisoned for life on Robben Island. He was doomed to work in irons in the slate quarries.

(IN BACKGROUND, VERY SOFTLY, XHOSA DIRGE)

It is melancholy to reflect how valuable an instrument for promoting the civilisation of the Caffer tribes was lost by the nefarious treatment of that extraordinary barbarian, whom a wiser and more generous policy might have rendered a grateful ally to the colony, and a permanent benefactor to his own countrymen.

NARRATOR:	A year later, Makana and some 30 others who were imprisoned on the Island, overpowered and disarmed the guards, seized a boat and made their escape. By some mischance the pinnace was upset. Several who escaped relate that Makana clung for some time to a rock, and that his deep sonorous voice was heard loudly cheering on those who were struggling with the billows, until he was swept off and engulfed by the raging surf.

(SEA)

During the 1830s the war against the British entered a new phase: Chief Maqoma, 'The giant of the Ngqika tribe,' led the tribes. But, defeated by superior arms and organisation, he was demoralised.

In 1847 he encountered the new Governor of the Cape, Sir Harry Smith, who announced to a gathering of Chiefs and tribesmen that henceforth they would be ruled by Queen Victoria.

SIR HARRY SMITH:	I spoke in a very impressive manner. Then I allowed each Chief to come forward and kiss my foot. Maqoma offered me his hand. Whereupon I forced him to the ground, put a foot on his neck, and brandished a sword over his head, while upbraiding him for his misconduct.
NARRATOR:	Before long Maqoma was conducting a brilliant guerrilla campaign against the Colonists but, defeated again, he and six other chiefs were sentenced to transportation to Robben Island, for 20 years. In 1875, Maqoma, then in his seventies, died on the Island.

Thirty years earlier, in 1844, in Despatch number 141, the British planned the removal to Robben Island of 'chronic sick, lunatics and paupers' of all races. Men and women. Among the chronic sick were lepers. Among the insane: many found guilty of criminal assault.

Orgies embarrassed the authorities who fought a losing battle against the smuggling of dagga and liquor. On a night of dense fog, a ship was wrecked and in the flotsam washed up were barrels of whisky. Lepers came running, and convicts were brought under guard to clear the wreckage. As kegs smashed against rocks, lepers and convicts knelt to suck up the whisky.

Guards rounded them all up and marched them, staggering and singing happily, back to their wards and cells.

By the 1860s the insane predominated among the four-hundred patients.
Those who tried to escape: if they were not captured, drowned or died of exposure.

When Governor Sir Philip Wodehouse visited the Island, he liked the place. Among the paupers was a rheumatic woman, Mrs Brown, and her daughter Christiana. In a letter to one of the numerous Commissions which ineffectually investigated conditions, Christiana wrote:

CHRISTIANA:
Robben Island, November 1861.
Gentlemen,
To attempt the showing forth of my own inconveniences is exceedingly repulsive to my feelings, but I consider it my duty to take some part in showing what the evils of this establishment consist in. I will lay before you a few of the things which trouble myself and my mother. Our first and greatest objection is the disgusting company by which we are surrounded; and not only are we obliged to meet them continually outside our dwelling, but also to dwell with them in the same room, and to be continually annoyed with their conversation which is always uncongenial of its nature, coarse in its quality, and frequently are our ears polluted by blasphemous remarks and obscene jests. Alarm and vexation are ever being excited, often by the sudden intrusion of a lunatic into our room. I cannot altogether forget that they are likely to commit acts of violence. Then, who can meet lepers face to face without disgust and is it not oppressive to the spirits to be surrounded by the blind, the lame, the deaf, the idiot, those suffering from loathsome sores and, worst of all, the confirmed and hardened drunkard. Truly this Island is a land of darkness and of the shadow of death.
I am, yours truly, Christiana Brown.

(SEA)

NARRATOR:
In 1873, in Natal, Langalibalele, Chief of a minor amaHlubi tribe, after a minor disagreement with the British, attempted to escape their jurisdiction. His flight, with his tribes and cattle, was regarded as treason. British troops pursued him and in the ensuing skirmish, three Englishmen were killed. Langalibalele was captured and imprisoned. A powerful and persistent voice spoke up: John Colenso, Bishop of Natal:

COLENSO:
The Chief has been kept in solitary confinement. When I attempted to secure an advocate, he was not allowed to see the Chief or to lend any assistance at his trial.

COLONIST'S WIFE:
Why should the Bishop insist that justice be done to black and white alike? It is the grossest bad taste in a clergyman.

COLENSO:
The tribe has been outlawed. More than 200, including old men, women and children, have been killed. Two thousand have been captured. Their lands confiscated, their property seized, thousands of huts burned down.

NARRATOR:
And their chief, Langalibalele, was sentenced to be transported to Robben island – for life.

COLENSO:
Through this policy the name of Englishman is fast becoming in the native mind the synonym for duplicity, treachery and violence, instead of – as in days gone by – for truth and justice and righteousness.

COLONIST:
The Bishop's obstinate persistence! And to say that English treatment of the native races is little better than a tissue of mistakes, blunders and crimes!

NARRATOR:
Disregarding hints that he might be lynched or tarred and feathered, Colenso, an old man, exhausted by years when he himself had been persecuted for his unorthodox religious views, now spent all his energy in trying to secure justice. He went back and forth to London, appealing to the Government, to the Queen. On a Friday morning in January 1875 he took the steamer to Robben Island.

95

COLENSO:	The passage took about 45 minutes. We were landed from the little steamer in a boat, from which we got into chairs carried between staves on the shoulders of convicts. It is perfectly inhuman in any Christian Government to have sent the Chief and his son to this spot, where they have had no one to speak to of their own kind, and have endured this misery month after month. They were of course rejoiced to see me with, so they fondly hoped, a word of grace from the Queen for them. I had to tell them, I did not know when they would be removed from Robben Island. 'Then it is death for us,' said the Chief, and drew his finger across his throat.
NARRATOR:	Langalibalele was removed to the mainland some months later. It was 12 years before he was allowed to return to Natal. He was still a prisoner, and by then a pauper.
	In 1913 the insane were removed to the mainland and in 1931, the lepers. An evangelist who had visited the hundreds of lepers between 1904 and 1920 was the Rev. James Fish. In his diary he said:
	18 November 1904: Oh, how little one can do among over 600 lepers, scattered over the Island, with the few hours at our disposal. I was impressed with a sight that I shall not soon forget – four native women huddled together in a little tin hut, about five foot square, their poor bodies mutilated. I beckoned Messrs. Elliot and Sharp to come near, but at once the poor things shrank back with shame and protested, and although I assured them of our fullest sympathy, they still drew back. It struck me that, after all, deeper than the black skin, there was clearly manifested the delicate feelings which belong to women. My companions were interested in watching a woman kneeling before a tub and washing clothes, although she was without hands, having just the two stumps.
	28 July 1905: I was grieved and disappointed to find that the girl Maggie, of whom I had great hopes, now turns out to be a Roman Catholic at heart.
	July 1922: Today a Faith Healer visited the Island. It was most impressive to witness 200 poor afflicted people hobbling and crawling to the Church to have his hands laid upon them. There are heart-rending scenes on that Island. It is there one understands a little of what 'The groaning creation' means.
NARRATOR:	During the Second World War, the Island – cleaned up – was used by the South African Navy and, in 1959 in the South African House of Assembly, the Minister of Justice, B J Vorster announced: 'The Government has decided to hand over Robben Island to the Department of Prisons. We intend to take it over to provide a maximum security institution'. 'A local Alcatraz!' Quipped a member of the Opposition. 'Yes', said Vorster,'not a Devil's Island'. Robben Island: Maximum Security prison. The surrounding ocean dangerous, with strong currents. The jail blocks said to be impregnable. But the rare visitors permitted by the government had a pleasing impression: gum trees had been planted, deer and ostrich introduced, the yellow-blossomed bushes still flourished – as did the penguins and the rabbits. And the quarries.
	Since 1963 most black political prisoners – the men, that is – have served long sentences on the Island. Many, like Andimba ja Toivo from Namibia, had been tortured before being brought to trial. Who were these men? What were their jobs? They were lawyers, teachers, factory workers, labourers, clerks, students, trade unionists. Their offences? Those sentenced to life had been found guilty of organising sabotage or taking part in guerrilla activity. Eddie Daniels, sentenced for sabotage along with young white liberals, served 15 years while his white comrades were released after two years.
AFRICAN PRISONER 1:	Most, like me, were sentenced for 'furthering the aims' of a banned organisation – the African National Congress or the Pan Africanist Congress.
NARRATOR:	Such sentences were particularly heavy in the Eastern Cape – the land of Makana and Maqoma. Charges were often broken down under multiple counts: for instance, one man who gave a donation to the ANC, who allowed his house to be used for a meeting and who distributed three leaflets – was sentenced to ten years.

96

AFRICAN PRISONER 2:	Myself, for four years. I do not deny that I took part in ANC activities, but all the same, the evidence given against me in court was fabricated. On 5 January 1965, with others from Port Elizabeth, I was put in chains and transferred in two fully-packed trucks. Most had to stand all the way, hundreds of miles, until we reached Cape Town. One had to urinate where one was, there being no chance of manoeuvering one's way to the bucket at the back of the truck. We didn't have any food. At the docks we were bundled into the hold of a ferry. It was the first time I rode in a boat. The first time I saw the sea – and it was rough! Many of us were seasick.

(SOFTLY IN BACKGROUND SOUND OF SEA AND GULLS)

AFRICAN PRISONER 1:	It was in August 1964 that I made my journey as a bondman to the Island – this devil island, place of the martyrs, which we called Makana Island. When we trod its soil I jerked my head and saw Table Mountain, appearing in pomp and beauty – the mountain that saw the ships of the navigators, that witnessed the landing of Van Riebeeck and his group, so that today the indigenous of this land are accursed by the follies of history. Because of that, I found myself in this place, a prisoner.
AFRICAN PRISONER 2:	You know, we saw thousands of human skeletons, unearthed when foundations for a building were dug – generations of prisoners who died there, lepers too.
NARRATOR:	One man, Robert Sobukwe, leader of the Pan Africanist Congress, was not sentenced at all. Flown to the island in April 1963, he was detained without trial under a special law passed by Parliament. Guarded by warders and by dogs, he lived alone in a two-roomed bungalow surrounded by a high barbed-wire fence. He spent his days reading or studying, gardening or staring at Table Mountain. Year after year after year the Minister of Justice renewed the detention order. Prisoners were not permitted near Sobukwe's cottage. When they glimpsed him in the distance —
AFRICAN PRISONER 1:	It was a great inspiration to us!
NARRATOR:	Of about 1 300 prisoners more than 1 000 had been found guilty of political offenses – 'crimes against the state' was the official term. The rest were common law prisoners.
AFRICAN PRISONER 2:	All the warders were white. They greeted us:
WARDER 1:	You've been claiming South Africa! The Government has accordingly decided to concede and grant you the Island.
WARDER 2:	*Hier julle gaan vrek!* The motto is: Less food, less trouble. Enjoy your stay! *God, hier's 'n koelie hier!*
INDIAN PRISONER 1:	Sir, we are not coolies.
WARDER 1:	There's no 'sir' on the Island, only *'Baas'*.
INDIAN PRISONER 1:	Batons rained down on us.
NARRATOR:	Dennis Brutus, the poet, was given an extra beating because:
WARDER 2:	*Hy is die ou wat skuldig is, hy het ons uit die Olympik spele geskors!*

(SCUFFLE AS PRISONERS TRY TO ESCAPE BLOWS)

AFRICAN PRISONER 1:	A warder counted us. He repeated the count several times without getting the correct total.

(PRISONERS TALK AMONG THEMSELVES)

WARDER 1:	Keep quiet! I can't hear myself counting!

(LOUD LAUGHTER)

Thula! Kom! Kom!

AFRICAN PRISONER 1:	We were marched to the cells ...
AFRICAN PRISONER 2:	There was a section of large cells which held about 60 prisoners each ...
AFRICAN PRISONER 1:	Seventy, the one I was in ...
NARRATOR:	Then there was segregation section – single cells where Nelson Mandela, Walter Sisulu and others of the Rivonia group were among those imprisoned ... Mandela, during their trial in 1964, admitted that he had organised sabotage. In explaining why he had turned to violence, he told the court:
MANDELA:	Africans want to be paid a living wage. Africans want to perform work they are capable of doing and not work which the Government declares them to be capable of. Africans want to live where they obtain work and not be endorsed out of an area because they were not born there. We want to be part of the general population, and not confined to living in ghettos. African men want to have their wives and children to live with them where they work and not be forced into an unnatural existence in men's hostels. African women want to be with their menfolk and not left permanently widowed in the Reserves. We want to be allowed to travel in our own country. We want a just share in the whole of South Africa. We want security and a stake in society. Above all, we want equal political rights, because without them our disabilities will be permanent. This then is what the African National Congress is fighting for. It is a struggle of the African people, inspired by their own suffering and their own experience. It is a struggle for the right to live.

(IN BACKGROUND VERY SOFTLY, XHOSA DIRGE)

NARRATOR:	Mandela and the other Rivonia men were sentenced to life imprisonment. Handcuffed and chained by the ankles, they were flown to Robben Island. The cells in the segregated section were about seven foot square, lit by a 40-watt bulb, on the floor a sisal mat and roll of threadbare blankets. Dennis Brutus was in that section:
BRUTUS:	Cement-grey floors and walls Cement-grey days Cement-grey time and a grey susurration as of seas breaking winds blowing and rains drizzling. A barred existence So that one did not need to look at doors or windows to know that they were sundered by bars and one locked in a grey gelid stream of unmoving time.
NARRATOR:	It was mid-winter and the North-Wester often lashed the Island. The regulation shorts and shirt, thin jersey and jacket gave no protection against the bitter cold.

(LOUD CLANGING OF BELL)

AFRICAN PRISONER 2:	The Island day by day: Monday to Friday we were woken at 5.30. Breakfast was mealie-pap with a teaspoon of sugar, half a pint of black coffee and what they called soup. By 7.15 all spans had to be out of the yard. Criminals had the better jobs – working for warders in their houses, say. Most political prisoners from the big cells laboured at the stone quarry, right near a beach. A huge hole since generations of prisoners had been digging there.

AFRICAN PRISONER 1:	I was taken to the quarry on bare feet. The stones were sharp, they cut deep into the flesh.
AFRICAN PRISONER 2:	Eventually we were given crude sandals or shoes. Mine were old, the one a different size from the other, and both not my correct size. One had a heel three inches high – when we went to the quarry we were supposed to trot – it was most awkward.

(LAUGHTER)

(CRIES OF SEAGULLS BEHIND WHAT FOLLOWS)

INDIAN PRISONER 1:	Hundreds of us sat in a huge circle, hammers flying up and down. We had to split rocks into small stones; others had to push wheelbarrows laden with rocks or drill holes in the rockface. Warders constantly walked past, beating, shouting.
WARDER 2:	*Daardie vark! Jy, werk man werk!*

(MEN COMPLAIN IN LOW VOICES)

WARDER 2:	*Julle maak raas daarso! Drie maaltye more!*
AFRICAN PRISONER 1:	We called our span the hodoshe span. Hodoshe was the name we gave our span warder —it's a Xhosa name for the big green fly that feasts on human faeces. He knew his nickname – he did not know its meaning!
NARRATOR:	All but the leaders were liable to be assaulted. Andrew Masondo, university lecturer, was beaten up, his left shoulder broken.
INDIAN PRISONER 1:	Warders seemed to enjoy seeing us suffer – to them we were not human.
AFRICAN PRISONER 2:	In summer the sun scorched mercilessly.
NARRATOR:	As the men heaved and strained Johnson Mlambo protested. One of the warders ordered common law prisoners to dig a deep hole and bury him up to his neck. Hours later the warder approached him.
WARDER 2:	(IN GREAT GOOD HUMOUR) *Kaffir, soek jy water? Nee, ek sal jou nie water gee nie, ek sal jou die beste brandewyn gee!*

(RAUCOUS LAUGHTER OF SEVERAL WARDERS)

NARRATOR:	And he urinated at Mlambo's mouth. Later Mlambo was dug out. He washed the earth off and joined his comrades, not saying a word.
INDIAN PRISONER 1:	His silence was terrible and there was nothing we could say to him.
NARRATOR:	When prisoners complained they were punished, but affidavits eventually reached Mrs Helen Suzman and were quoted by her in Parliament and in the press overseas. A new Commandant was sent to the Island and two or three warders were removed. But this Commandant was soon replaced by a man nicknamed Staalbaard —
AFRICAN PRISONER 1:	— a real pig – then came a big brute who hit indiscriminately with his cane. But there were improvements in his term – long pants in winter.
NARRATOR:	Next came a CO who actually listened to complaints. But whatever the changes of staff, certain things recur in prisoners' testimonies. Kulukudu for instance – solitary confinement on spare diet – a punishment for protesting or not working hard enough. As for medical callousness or laxity, to mention one case described by a Namibian: Petrus Nailenge was so ill with TB that he was taken to Cape Town for treatment only to be returned to the Island hospital in a worse condition. Yet his comrades were not allowed to visit him and alone he died.

AFRICAN PRISONER 2:	In winter there was often that drizzle that could wet a cat to the skin and leave it cringing from the freezing air of the Antarctic.
AFRICAN PRISONER 1:	On days of dense mist we heard that strangled noise —

(LONG DRAWN-OUT SOUND OF FOGHORN)

We never got used to it, the sickening lowe of a dying cow, and the echo would carry very far.

NARRATOR:	It was in winter that Mandela and most of the men in the segregation section, after a year of breaking stones in the yard, were formed into a span and ordered to head for the lime quarry. One of the Rivonia men has described that first occasion —
RIVONIA MAN:	In jail warders are used to rushing people, and they tried to do that with us.
WARDER 1:	*Vas! Vas!*
RIVONIA MAN:	Nelson, at the front, set the pace, walking very slowly. That became very effective. The warder was following us up from the back and ran to the front to plead with him. From that day they recognized there was leadership and they would have to talk to the leader – we were all happy about that.
NARRATOR:	The lime quarry was near the centre of the Island. The glare was intense – men argued that they needed sun-glasses but these were said to be useless.
RIVONIA MAN:	Working with pick-axes and spades we sang, it's the easy way to gain energy, we were singing freedom songs and those songs labourers working on roads sing —

(MEN SING SUCH A RHYTHMICAL SONG)

WARDERS 1 & 2:	*Thula! Thula!*

(SINGING CONTINUES)

RIVONIA MAN:	The following day they said no more singing —
AFRICAN PRISONER 2:	We from the big cells, we were allowed to sing. In the stone quarry where you needed ropes and chains to pull heavy loads you could only do it if you sang – but whistling? Never!
RIVONIA MAN:	When we went on singing, warders brought four common law prisoners to the lime quarry to try and provoke us. They sang in mockery, 'What were you doing at Rivonia?' And one of us, from high up in the quarry, sang, 'Ketayako – Choose your path —'
	(CHANTING SONG OF COMMON LAW MEN DROWNED AS THE SOLOIST IS JOINED BY THE OTHER POLITICALS)
RIVONIA MAN:	We came back to the cells tired, our hands blistered. For many weeks it was very painful. And it was terrible undressing – so cold and we had to wash in icy water – we were filthy with lime-dust and sweat.
	One day at the quarry we were asked: all those who have drivers' licenses, stand to one side! We thought we would be driving the lorries, so all of us who could drive, stood aside. And we were given wheel-barrows to push!

(LOUD LAUGHTER)

NARRATOR:	Now food —
WOMAN OFFICIAL:	Diets for prisoners are prescribed by professional dieticians of the Department of Health – a specimen diet scale for lunch —

AFRICAN PRISONER 1:	(INTERRUPTING) Our lunch consisted of mealies and a half pint —
WOMAN OFFICIAL:	— meat seven ounces, vegetables twelve ounces —
AFRICAN PRISONER 2:	Meat! Three or four days a week only two ounces, small pieces you wouldn't even give your cat!
WOMAN OFFICIAL:	Supper: Protone soup powder one ounce, vegetables —
AFRICAN PRISONER 1:	— a sort of powder, *phuzamandla*, it's to drink, they are saying, you know, it's for to keep you healthy. Lunchtime, they put beans with stones in the mealies, one time a fellow went to the authorities, he said: 'Look, we don't mind you cooking stones, but these stones must be cooked well'. It's what he said, that was a joke!
WOMAN OFFICIAL:	(DRONING ON) Bread eight ounces. Milk, a minimum daily issue —
AFRICAN PRISONER 2:	Oh no! Bread! Milk! Is that what they tell the world?
NARRATOR:	Only Indian and coloured prisoners were allowed bread.
WOMAN OFFICIAL:	Salads are served twice weekly.
AFRICAN PRISONER 1:	Good God! (GUFFAWS) 1967 we got oranges! Yes, one time, it was on a Saturday.
NARRATOR:	And three ounces of fish on Thursdays. The nightly soup —
COLOURED PRISONER:	— tasted like poison!
NARRATOR:	Locked in the cells in late afternoon —
AFRICAN PRISONER 1:	In the big cells we had very good choirs.
INDIAN PRISONER 1:	The concerts were illegal; instead of clapping we would rub our hands together.
PRISONERS:	(SINGING — IN ZULU) We are the brown nation We are yearning for our land We yearn for our land That has been taken by the white man. We, the sons of Africa, We are yearning for our land. Let them leave our land ... (SOUND OF 40 PAIRS OF HANDS RUBBING)
RIVONIA MAN:	In the segregation section we were not supposed to sing at all!
BRUTUS:	Nothing was sadder there was no more saddening want than the deadly lack of music ... it grew to a hunger — the bans on singing, whistling — and unappreciative ears made it worse. Then those who shared one's loves and hungers grew more dear on this account — Fiks and Jeff and Neville and the others. Strains of *Eine Kleine Nacht Musik* — (VOICE FADES AS MEN, ONE AFTER ANOTHER, VERY QUIETLY WHISTLE A FEW BARS)

Surreptitious wisps of melody
down the damp grey concrete corridors.
Joy.

NARRATOR:	The authorities tried to cut political prisoners off from all news of the outside world. Letters were heavily censored, family matters only, 500 words the limit. Occasionally newspapers were smuggled to them by common law prisoners who cleaned warders' homes.
RIVONIA MAN:	We were not choosy – to us there was no such thing as stale news – it might be a year old, it was digested with relish.
NARRATOR:	And each new prisoner was enthusiastically questioned.
AFRICAN WIFE:	After my husband had been on the Island six months I was given permission to visit him. There was so much excitement, the children all wanted to come.
NARRATOR:	Children under 18 were not allowed to visit their fathers. This woman, by the way, was a doctor. Her husband also was a doctor.
AFRICAN WIFE:	During the long journey from Johannesburg by train, you can imagine, one was in high excitement all the way. At the docks, strict security. In my ignorance I'd brought some sandwiches for him, these were confiscated. About 15 others were there, amongst them Albertina Sisulu and Winnie Mandela. I was in a boat for the first time! Some got sick but I was joyously expectant. But as the boat took a turn to go in towards the Island's dock, it became very cold – a sudden chilling wind – I thought, oh my God it is here these men are, some of them for a lifetime. There were harsh commands. Ashore we were marched to a building, along a narrow passage and into little cubicles.
AFRICAN HUSBAND:	We would talk about the visit we were expecting – about a week before, there'd be an air of expectancy. We would jot down notes of what to say. Fellow-prisoners would ask us to send messages. Your name is called, you are marched along. Warders seemed to go out of their way to be nasty, sometimes by the time you met your visitor you'd be in a vile temper. We'd be lined up in the cubicles with glass windows. As soon as the visitors came in we were all straining to see who was there.
AFRICAN WIFE:	Through the glass I could see my husband. I wanted to run to him, to hold him, but there was this wall between us. I hurried to the glass. Oh, I was shocked – he was very thin and quite different, in only six months!
AFRICAN HUSBAND:	We had not seen a woman for so long, it was quite an experience – they all looked so pretty!
AFRICAN WIFE:	We began a rather funny conversation – warders were there and we'd been warned we mustn't say anything outside family matters. It became unnatural. (TO AFRICAN HUSBAND) How are you?
AFRICAN HUSBAND:	I'm all right. How are the children?
AFRICAN WIFE:	No, they're fine. They send love. (TO AUDIENCE) We went on like that.
AFRICAN HUSBAND:	I forgot the notes – try to remember all the messages but my state of excitement made it difficult. The half hour was nearly up. (TO WIFE) Pass my love to the children and kiss them.
AFRICAN WIFE:	We were literally crying.
WARDER 1:	Time up!
AFRICAN WIFE:	We hung around a little, watched them being marched away, their thinness. Albertina said, 'Oh, our men are shrinking here! But their spirit is so strong!'
AFRICAN HUSBAND:	You are marched back to the cells. Already it's like a dream, did it happen? So many things you wanted to say ...

AFRICAN WIFE:	We were marched straight back to the boat. We were different people altogether. No conversation, each one absorbed, crying quietly to herself. Then the 1000 mile journey back home.
AFRICAN PRISONER 2:	Afterwards, the visited prisoner assumed an aura of unusual importance, his fellows plying him with questions. There were those who had no visits ever. Elderly men, some of them, illiterate peasants. Nobody knew of their families to donate money for the fares. Some had completely lost track of their families – the forced removals, you know. They were forgotten people, completely despondent.
NARRATOR:	Over the years Robert Sobukwe's wife and family were occasionally permitted to visit him. And Mrs Suzman, during a visit to the Island, was escorted to his cottage by the CO and several warders.
MRS SUZMAN:	We shook hands and I said, 'I'm Helen Suzman. How are you, Mr Sobukwe?' He replied: 'I am forgetting how to speak.' The reply startled me. I just looked at him. 'Well, whom do I have to speak to?' he said.

(SOUND OF THE SEA AND GULLS)

NARRATOR:	Year after year after year men laboured on in the quarries. One lunch break in the stone quarry food ran out. Quite spontaneously a group of men went on hunger strike.
INDIAN PRISONER 1:	There was fear of what the repercussions might be and concern about how we could get word to the outside world. We had heard of force-feeding in British gaols, and of prisoners dying – how long could we stand it?
SENIOR WARDER:	It's your bloody business if you don't want to eat, I don't care a damn but you'll still work!
NARRATOR:	Others joined in and day after day, despite the fears, the hunger – and the temptation as the daily rations were suddenly much improved – the strike continued.
INDIAN PRISONER 1:	The news came through that the comrades in the segregation section, led by Nelson Mandela, as well as those in the Namibian section, had joined the strike. At night we sang with even more intensity than usual.
NARRATOR:	By the fifth day in the stone quarry their strength was failing, they felt isolated, they could only labour slowly.
INDIAN PRISONER 1:	Yet the majority were in favour of continuing, we recalled the long strikes of martyrs such as Mahatma Gandhi.
NARRATOR:	On the sixth day under a blazing sun more and more men were collapsing – suddenly a senior officer drove up —
SENIOR WARDER:	Well, what are your complaints!

(MEN ALL SHOUT AT ONCE)

AFRICAN PRISONER 2:	The end of assaults!
AFRICAN PRISONER 1:	... better, warmer clothing!
INDIAN PRISONER 1:	We demand to be recognised as political prisoners.
COLOURED PRISONER:	We too are human beings, we have feelings...
SENIOR WARDER:	All right, all right, elect three or four people and let's have a proper discussion.
NARRATOR:	The number of assaults fell and the warders' attitude was better, for a while the food improved.

INDIAN PRISONER 1:	How permanent the gains would be we did not know. And later the so-called ringleaders were sentenced to six months extra imprisonment. But whatever the authorities did to us, they could never take away our sense of victory.
NARRATOR:	After 15 years in the segregation section Eddie Daniels said:
DANIELS:	The government had two aims, to destroy our morale and to get the world to forget us. They failed dismally. Because being in the company of Mandela and Sisulu, instead of being weakened, they lifted you, they made you strong.
NARRATOR:	In the lime quarry, while digging and shovelling, the men managed to carry on classes: for instance Sisulu taught the history of the ANC, Mandela law, and Govan Mbeki not only economics but, he recalls:
MBEKI:	I started with one group when they were illiterate. By the time they left the Island they were able to write letters home – and they spoke English. Now Eddie Daniels, when he came there he was starved of education. But when he left he had a BA and a B Comm.
NARRATOR:	And Sisulu:
SISULU:	I did GCE and part of a BA but lost my studies five or six times – once because I was using my study material to record my letters home.
NARRATOR:	Losing studies, sometimes for years, was a worse punishment than solitary confinement. And political prisoners were banned from any creative writing – even memoirs. Mandela was punished when warders discovered autobiographical material he had buried in the exercise yard. Only Robert Sobukwe was allowed to write stories and poems. And was prevented from taking these with him when, in 1969, he was eventually released from the Island.

(SOUND OF THE SEA)

RIVONIA MAN:	It must have been in 1977 that our labouring in the lime quarry ended. Ordered to 'Fall in!', we were sent to a rocky beach to collect seaweed for fertiliser. A tough and dirty job. The sea was icy. And there were millions of small flies. But we had a good view of Cape Town – you fall in love with it, you cry and dream about South Africa and that city really represents home — very near yet very far.
INDIAN PRISONER 1:	Sometimes in the stone quarry as we were pushing barrows or chopping stones, we would notice something moving in the sea and there would be a whale. Or porpoises – we loved watching them, free and playful.
RIVONIA MAN:	At the beach we could collect mussels, *perlemoen*, crayfish, and with sea water in a rusty tin we'd boil them. One day the head of prison caught us at it. He tasted a mussel, pronounced it *'smaaklik'* – and that was it! No confrontation.
NARRATOR:	Repeated protests by deputations, through go-slow or hunger strikes, were winning improvements – from cold sea-water showers to fresh hot water, from stinking buckets to flush toilets. As for food: bread for all and eventually eggs.
RIVONIA MAN:	Eight eggs a week! As it was so many years since we'd had eggs we eagerly ate them, until the doctor advised not more than four. Then we got a consignment of peaches – we might have been a colony of Adams in the garden of Eden tasting the forbidden fruit!
NARRATOR:	On the whole, however, according to a new arrival in the big cells, the food was 'quite disagreeable'. Meanwhile letters and visits had been increased – but censorship remained strict. And newspapers were still prohibited.
RIVONIA MAN:	Common law prisoners had been moved from the Island but we managed to pilfer newspapers — in winter, for instance, when a warder had one tucked in the pocket of his greatcoat – or we might raid a rubbish dump —

INDIAN PRISONER 1:	We even got hold of a transistor radio! Until warders discovered it. The punishment was six strokes of a cane.
NARRATOR:	Not until 1980, through the intervention of the International Red Cross, were newspapers permitted.
RIVONIA MAN:	Sometimes we called them window papers because the censor had cut so much out. Eventually that was relaxed.
NARRATOR:	The most depressing news a man could get was unhappy news about his family – what could he do but suffer in his helplessness?
AFRICAN PRISONER 3:	My wife's life was almost destroyed by my imprisonment. You need your family, you need love, you are not in politics because you are loveless. You love people but the problem is apartheid. There is no life under apartheid, there is no love under apartheid. I want freedom so that I should see the result of our sufferings.
INDIAN PRISONER 3:	New arrivals were heartily welcomed – they brought inside information about the struggle, about the uprising of the youth in 1976 and the work being done in the outside world. Our morale was greatly boosted by knowing that we were not forgotten and that our leaders were honoured throughout the world. And we got news about our comrades – who had married, who was divorced, who was in prison.
NARRATOR:	And who had died. Through the years the men held rituals, mourning for – but also celebrating the lives of – those who had been hanged or killed in detention, among them Ahmed Timol and Steve Biko; and Chief Albert Lutuli, killed by a train; Ruth First and Griffiths and Victoria Mxenge, assassinated; as well as those who died of cancer – Bram Fischer while serving a life sentence and Robert Sobukwe while confined under bans and house arrest in Kimberley.
	(MEN SING SONG OF MOURNING WHICH RISES TO POWERFUL ENDING)
	One of the Rivonia men, in a letter written at Christmas after many years on the Island, said,
INDIAN PRISONER 2:	I cannot help but think back constantly to my last Christmas outside. I suppose more than any other class of people we cling tenaciously to the past and place our hopes and confidence in the future.
NARRATOR:	Meanwhile, a group of women in Cape Town had set up Cowley House to welcome and accommodate families on their way to visit prisoners. And on the Island men were creating gardens in the yards – Mac Maharaj, Laloo Chiba and Mandela smuggled in vegetable plants and soon had a bumper crop of tomatoes. While a PAC leader, Jeff Masemola, sculpted tribal figures with dog and buck outside the section where he was held.
INDIAN PRISONER 2:	One morning the boilers broke down. In the segregation section we got no meals and were kept locked in our cells all day. After angry protests, food was brought into the yard at ten o'clock at night and the cell doors were unlocked. We filed out. Hungry though we were, we ignored the food. For the first time in years we were seeing the night sky, the Milky Way, the Southern Cross – all of us gazing up, marvelling.
NARRATOR:	Govan Mbeki was the first to be given a bed. Eventually men in the other sections, now 30 to a cell, had beds. And Mbeki was the first to buy a guitar.
MBEKI:	It was wonderful – we taught ourselves and played pop songs from the African market.
INDIAN PRISONER 1:	One prisoner in our cell had an obsession: he picked up seaweed and hid it, with pieces of metal, zinc, cork and wire. There would be a raid and the warders would walk off with everything. He started collecting again and we saw him carving the seaweed and cutting holes in it. Every now and then he raised it to his lips and blew and we heard strange sounds.

(POSSIBLY HAVE THE STRANGE SOUND INSTEAD OF
"We heard the strange sounds"?)

Again the warders raided and stamped on this strange-looking object. He just started all over again. Slowly we saw what was emerging – a saxophone! More than a year passed before he managed to buy a reed from outside, then a totally new sound emerged, much richer and more varied.

He never stopped perfecting it, trying to make it more beautiful with silver paper. We loved it almost as much as its maker did. When visitors came the warders would show with great pride the amazing saxophone produced by their policy of encouraging artistic expression amongst the prisoners!

NARRATOR: One night two particular visitors were observed by men from the big cells.

INDIAN PRISONER 1: At the quarry that day we'd been surprised when the commanding officer asked if we wished to see a film. Surprised! No, astounded. And when we were locked up at five in our cells we felt anxious because the usual routine had been interrupted. We tried to smarten ourselves up, smooth our hair, but still we laughed at ourselves and said we were wasting our time, there would be no movie. But just before eight o'clock the warders came and we joined prisoners filing out of the other cells. The CO stood at the entrance to the hall with two men we had never seen before and he spoke to us in an unusually polite manner.

SENIOR WARDER: Hello, how are you?

INDIAN PRISONER 1: I was taken aback but replied that I was well, thank you. We saw a big Western movie. It was terrible, and we loved it. Half-way through the CO announced that we would be getting film shows once a month and we would be able to play sports – we couldn't believe our ears. On the way out he asked if we enjoyed the show and said good night. Next day we were introduced to the visitors – they were from the Red Cross in Geneva! We raised all our complaints about food, clothing, work, visits, censorship, medical treatment....

RIVONIA MAN: Among the movies we saw were *The French Connection, The Godfather, Kung Fu, Midnight Express.* Afterwards we discussed film technique and aesthetics. We thought Marlon Brando quite an actor – although we couldn't always make out what he was saying.

NARRATOR: They even saw *The Great Escape!*

RIVONIA MAN: Not much use to us!

NARRATOR: In the 400 year history of the Island only a handful tried to escape and most were drowned in those rough seas or easily captured. As for deaths on the Island, the only visible reminders are the leper cemetery and a shrine in memory of the Muslim sheiks and princes exiled from the East Indies during the eighteenth century.

INDIAN PRISONER 2: When all labour was ended for those of us in the segregation section we studied, read and gardened or played games such as scrabble, chess, draughts, table tennis, klabberjas, monopoly – we had teams, with an annual competition, the prizes were sweets.

NARRATOR: And their yard became a volley ball or tennis court. Then, as the CO had promised men from the big cells, came soccer:

INDIAN PRISONER 1: Wearing blue prison jerseys Rangers were captained by Comrade Jacob Zuma who was serving 10 years, and in khaki shirts were the Bucks under Comrade Curnick Ndhlovu, who was serving 20. I was the referee. Almost all the 1000 prisoners were watching. Through the high windows in the segregation section were the faces of our leaders: Mandela, Sisulu, Kathrada, Maharaj and others. The game started scrappily, everyone just running everywhere, kicking the ball wildly. Some even missed the ball completely and everybody laughed, including me, even though I was the referee.

PRISONERS: Kick the bloody ball!
Shoot at the goal!
Open your eyes ref!
Take him off the field!

INDIAN PRISONER 1:	Many were watching football for the first time – when there were shots at goal there was great excitement. The players came off exhausted, but our feeling was one of elation.
NARRATOR:	Conflicts between ANC and PAC were resolved and they formed the Makana Football Association of nine teams, holding league and knock-out competitions. But the leaders in the segregation section could no longer enjoy watching – their windows had been blacked out. They protested, and at last they themselves were playing soccer on a rough field near the Island's airstrip.
RIVONIA MAN:	Even Walter Sisulu – then in his late sixties – was eager to take part. And scored a goal – he did not realise, or pretended not to, that we connived at this!
NARRATOR:	Annual concerts had become a feature, with choirs or soloists performing and when men were allowed to receive musical instruments from their families, James Mange – who incidentally turned to the Rastafarian faith while on the Island – started a band. He and other prisoners taught each other, and soon there were five bands.
	(PERHAPS USE ONE OF MANGE'S WHIPLASH BAND NUMBERS?)
	Walter Sisulu recalls one particular night, a night of extreme cold.
	(SOUND OF BOOTS TRAMPING DOWN CORRIDOR, RATTLE OF KEYS)
SISULU:	A squad of warders armed with batons suddenly raided our section —
WARDERS:	(HARSH ORDERS) *Stilte in die gang! Teen die muur! Trek uit!*
SISULU:	I was undressed and feeling unwell. They made me lie on the floor, arms stretched out, they were searching. I thought I'll be kept here until the morning, that's going to mean pneumonia and finally death – I was having such ideas. In other cells they were assaulting – Ja Toivo fought back and was severely beaten, there was blood in his cell and in some others. That's one of the days I can never forget. Ja Toivo was kept in punishment isolation for a long time. It happened just like that, for no reason!
NARRATOR:	Over the years Mandela and Sisulu and their fellow prisoners gradually educated some warders.
RIVONIA MAN:	They lock people up – at the college where they studied they'd been given all sorts of ideas about who we are – very *gevaarlik*, coming to kill – then they see us studying, or going to church. Eventually we talk, we influence.
INDIAN PRISONER 1:	One warder who spoke politely and referred to us by our full names, even secretly passed on a packet of cigarettes from time to time. There were two or three like him – they called us '*kêrels*' when other said 'Kaffirs', '*koelies*', '*hotnot*' – they were soon transferred!
RIVONIA MAN:	In his relations with prison officers, Nelson Mandela differentiated between senior and junior — with junior officers who knew their position, he was charming and fatherly. Some solicited advice from him in connection with their jobs or social problems. The top officers had to answer his attacks on the rotten administrative practices, they had to field critical questions: 'We demand political status. We demand to be released ...'
NARRATOR:	Men have described their feelings on being released after serving their sentences:
AFRICAN PRISONER 4:	I felt lukewarm mainly because I was leaving so many of my dear comrades behind. Excitement was also smothered by thoughts, confused and speculative: Where was I going? Would I be allowed to join my family? Was I to be banned or house arrested?
INDIAN PRISONER 1:	Someone comes up to me, 'Didn't you hear, comrade, you must go and collect your things?' And someone whispers, 'Don't forget, the struggle continues.' Another says, 'Look up my wife for me, tell her that I'm still going strong and to have courage.' One by one the prisoners give me a last hug, many crying. And for the first time since my torture, I am crying.

AFRICAN PRISONER 3:	I was at sixes and sevens: Where am I going to get money to support my kids? You know, before I went to prison I was not keen on politics – but then you feel proud, you've been telling the truth, that was why you were on the Island.
SISULU:	It was in April 1982, about six o'clock in the evening – the Commanding Officer came to our section:
SENIOR WARDER:	Pack your things!
NARRATOR:	He addressed Mandela and Sisulu, and three other Rivonia men – Ahmed Kathrada, Raymond Mhlaba and Andrew Mlangeni – by then they had served 18 years on the Island.
SISULU:	We couldn't think what was happening, we knew we were being sent somewhere; where, we didn't know. We were taken to Cape Town, then on by van – we still didn't know where. We were driven to a prison. We felt very bad leaving our comrades. But we hoped we were on our way to Johannesburg. The following day we learned we were in Pollsmoor.
NARRATOR:	Five years later Govan Mbeki, escorted by the head of prisons and an armed guard, was flown from the Island and driven to Pollsmoor.
MBEKI:	I was taken to a lavishly furnished lounge. Then Nelson came. He looked fine. He spoke of his talks with some of the Cabinet and indicated I was going to be released as a test case.
NARRATOR:	Two years later came the release of Sisulu and the other Rivonia men from Pollsmoor, then, in February 1990, Mandela was freed from Viktor Verster prison – nearly 28 years since his arrest in August 1962.
	Meanwhile, among some 400 still held on the Island were young men who'd spent two years on Death Row in Pretoria for an attack on an oil refinery – in 1983 their sentence had been commuted to life imprisonment. Under an amnesty agreement they expected to be released by the end of April 1990. When that did not happen they went on hunger strike. Several of them collapsed. After Walter Sisulu had returned to the Island to intervene with the authorities their release was negotiated.
AFRICAN PRISONER 2:	How did people cope? Well, we knew we'd got to win in the end. The freedom fighters, they used to say, 'Look, you can do anything but we are going to continue with our struggle.' Warders tried to foster this question of *'Baas'*. And we refused. The question of *'Baas'* did not exist in our minds.
BRUTUS:	It is not all terror and deprivation, you know; one comes to welcome the closer contact and understanding one achieves with one's fellow-men...
AFRICAN PRISONER 1:	It's one of the protective mechanisms of human nature, however adverse the conditions you will find something to laugh at. It was very funny, some things which today when I think of them were not so funny, we saw the humorous side!
AFRICAN PRISONER 2:	On the Island there were Africans, there were coloureds, there were Indians – among the Africans were Xhosas, Zulus, Tswana, Shangaan – of course there were quarrels, but on the whole, their friendship, you couldn't find it anywhere outside. They could use one spoon when they were eating. *Makavane* – just like that.
AFRICAN PRISONER 1:	*Makavane* means comrades.
INDIAN PRISONER 2:	And there was the support of our women – not just wives, but mothers!
AFRICAN PRISONER 3:	I was inspired by our leadership – people who have sacrificed for so many years. From them I took courage – after such trying times they have emerged unbroken, their love for freedom remains.

(SOUND OF SEA GROWING LOUD)

RIVONIA MAN: You know, that time we were banned from singing, on one day of the year we defied!
                June 16!

COLOURED PRISONER: Afrika Day!

(ALL SING NKOSI SIKELEL' I AFRIKA, DROWNING SOUND OF SEA)

(AS SINGING DIES AWAY)

NARRATOR: Today tourists and journalists visit the Island. From Cape Town docks the boat steams past
             seals on its way to the flat rocky outcrop. From the Island's jetty a coach conveys nature
             lovers in search of ostriches and bontebok, springbok and penguins. Journalists are officially
             conducted through the prison. They see the small cells in which Mandela and Sisulu and their
             comrades spent almost 20 years. The lime quarry remains a dazzling white monument and
             rainwater hides the depths of the stone quarry. Table Mountain appears tantalisingly close.
             All around the ocean threatens, its breakers thunder against the Island's shores. The cries of
             Makana, of Christiana Brown, of slaves and lepers and sheiks, resound in the imagination as
             do the powerful voices, the unexpected laughter and the singing of modern men who so
             arduously struggled for the freedom of their people.

Voices from Robben Island is a book with which we at Nedbank are proud to be associated.

It is being published at a time when the majority of South Africans are tasting true democracy for the first time. Like the video of the same name, which Nedbank is also supporting, the book's message of man's courage and strength in the face of unequal odds is relevant to the times we live in. It is also a powerful reminder to present and future generations to forgive the tragedies of the past, while at the same time never allow them to be repeated.

Voices from Robben Island bears testimony to the universal goodness of man; to the triumph of good over evil. Nedbank identifies with the educative merits and insights of this book and trusts that it will contribute to bringing about an awareness of the importance of human dignity, tolerance and understanding.

On behalf of all Nedbankers — our staff, clients and shareholders — I would like to wish everyone who was involved in producing this book, much success.

Finally, I would like to emphasise an important message which we at Nedbank support on an ongoing basis — the message of peace among all South Africans. We hope that, together with Nedbank, you will continue to find ways to spread this message. Our support of books like *Voices from Robben Island*, is one way of doing this.

NEDBANK